D. G Hubbard

## The Polyglot Pronouncing Hand-Book

A Key to the Correct Pronunciation of Current Geographical and other Proper

Names from Foreign Languages

D. G Hubbard

**The Polyglot Pronouncing Hand-Book**
*A Key to the Correct Pronunciation of Current Geographical and other Proper Names from Foreign Languages*

ISBN/EAN: 9783743394285

Manufactured in Europe, USA, Canada, Australia, Japa

Cover: Foto ©Paul-Georg Meister /pixelio.de

Manufactured and distributed by brebook publishing software (www.brebook.com)

D. G Hubbard

**The Polyglot Pronouncing Hand-Book**

# THE

# POLYGLOT

# PRONOUNCING HAND-BOOK.

## A Key

TO THE CORRECT PRONUNCIATION OF CURRENT GEOGRAPHICAL
AND OTHER PROPER NAMES FROM FOREIGN LANGUAGES.

BY

D. G. H. *Hubbard*

CHICAGO AND NEW YORK:

RAND, McNALLY & COMPANY, PUBLISHERS.

1890.

# PREFACE.

This little hand-book, though it may prove a welcome convenience to many a student, is not meant especially for the use of scholars. If it might choose a public, it would be the public of newspaper readers. Its aim is merely to tell to any one of that somewhat extended circle, how to pronounce perhaps nine out of ten of the names of persons or places the world over, to be met in the columns of English or American newspapers. Even this modest aim it does not claim to accomplish, in either extent or manner, perfectly. So small a book can not well give the means of so much as guessing at the sound of even nine-tenths of all the names in the world. No book can perfectly convey to persons who know only English, sounds that do not occur in English. This particular book does not profess to give, even by approximation, the sounds of any language in its entirety. As to the pronunciation of many languages, there are rules and exceptions which do not affect proper names, yet of which the statement or adequate illustration would occupy space that could be ill afforded in the plan of so compact and small a volume, while their omission would be seldom felt, even in a study of the language as a whole.

What the book does give, however, it claims to give promptly and simply, without much turning of leaves, without slow and doubtful interpretation of a complex system of phonetic symbols, and in a manner to be understood at a glance. In most languages of Europe, as also in those of other regions of the globe, from which names come before English-speaking readers with comparative uniformity of pronunciation, these names are classed according to the letters or combinations of letters occurring in them which have a value other than the English value. The name and its sound are close together; with possibly the exception of a single language, all the sounds of all the names in a language are placed at one glance before the eye, within the compass of one, or at most of two, small pages. Where the irregularity of pronunciation is too

411484

great for such classification, the names are arranged in alphabetical lists as comprehensive as they could well be made in accordance with the plan of the book.

In bespeaking indulgence for the inevitable short-comings of his book, the compiler must plead excuses, the full weight of which can be felt only by those who have been engaged in similar work. Even in so thoroughly finished and polished a language as the French he has not had the fortune to find a single grammar that gave the sounds of the language really exhaustive treatment, nor any two whose treatment of them agreed in all points. In the Slavic and other languages of Eastern Europe, as well as in those of other quarters of the world, not only is the unsettled condition of the pronunciation often made worse by the intermingling of distinct races on the same soil, but this double confusion is still worse confounded by the extreme carelessness of translators, through whose transliteration alone do names from these languages commonly come before English-speaking readers. There is no assurance that an English translator, for instance, may not use now English, now French, now German equivalents, and that, not merely in the same volume, but in the same word, and, if the word be long enough, in the same occurrence of that word. A Russian, translating from the Russian, may feel no obligation to any particular consistency of method in representing the sounds of his mother-tongue. Such considerations, the compiler trusts, may suffice to shield him from too large a share of responsibility for defects in his work, of which he is beforehand well aware, but which, he feels assured, will not prevent its proving a very useful and convenient hand-book.

# TABLE OF CONTENTS.

# THE POLYGLOT PRONOUNCING HAND-BOOK.

The mathematical sign of equality, =, throughout the book, expresses the equivalence of characters connected by it.

## FRENCH.

| | | | |
|---|---|---|---|
| a = a | in ah | Cannes | kahn |
| | | Barras | bah-rah' |
| am[1] = en | in encore | Chambéry | chahnh-bai-ree' |
| an[1] = en | in encore | Vauban | vo-bahnh' |
| e[2] = e | in battery | Chevreul | shŏ-vröl'[4] |
| | | Anquetil | ahnh-kŏ-teel' |
| e[3] = e | in ebb | Etienne | ā-tee-en' |
| | | Daguerre | dah-gherr' |
| é = ā | in ale | Crébillon | crā-bee-yonh' |
| | | Fénelon | fā-n[1]-lonh' |
| è = e | in there | Molière | mo-lee-air' |
| | | Ampère | ahm-pair' |
| en[1] = en | in encore | Argenteuil | arr-zhonh[7]-tö'-ee |
| | | Genlis | zhonh[7]-lee' |
| i = ee | in bee | Ivry | ee-vree' |
| | | Racine | rah-seen' |
| in[1] = an | in anchor | Ingré | ănh[6]-grā' |
| | | Bernardin | bair-nar-dănh'[6] |
| on[1] = on | in monk | Bourdon | bour-donh' |
| | | Gougon | goo-gonh' |
| u = ü[5] | | Bossu | bos-sü' |
| | | Bugeaud | bü-zhō'[7] |

1. After a vowel, *m* and *n*, when either final or followed by a consonant which is neither *m* nor *n*, have a nasal sound very like that of *n* in anchor, but somewhat less distinct. 2. *e* unaccented, if final, is mute; elsewhere, except as in next remark, is obscure, as in batter. 3. When unaccented and before a consonant in the same syllable. 4. ŏ represents, throughout the book, the obscure sound of *i* in *sir* or of *u* in *fur*. 5. *ü* represents, throughout the book, a sound unknown in English and which is perhaps most readily produced, if, while uttering a broad *ah* and without interrupting the sound, the lips and tongue are brought into position for whistling. Final consonants are silent, excepting *c*, *f*, *l*, and *r*. 6. ă = *a* in *Anne*. 7. *zh* = *z* in *leizure*.

(9)

## FRENCH—Continued.

| | | | |
|---|---|---|---|
| un = önh[1] | | Lebrun | lö-brönh′ |
| | | Yverdun | ee-vair-dönh′ |
| y = ee | in bee | Ivry | ee-vree′ |
| | | Yprés | ee-prä′ |
| ym ⎫ [1] ⎬ = an | in anchor | Drouyn | droo-ănh′[6] |
| yn ⎭ | | | |

1, 4, 6. See notes on preceding page.

---

| | | | |
|---|---|---|---|
| ae = ah | | Caen | kahnh |
| | | Stael | stahl |
| ai = ā | in ale | Aisne | āne |
| | | Montaigne | monh-tane′ |
| ai[1] = e | in there | Clairaut | clair-ō |
| ai[2] = ah-ee | | Baillet | bah-ee-yā′ |
| aim = an | in anchor | Etain | ā-tāhnh′ |
| ain | | Maintenon | mănh-t-nonh′ |
| ao = ō | in no | Saone | sōne |
| ao = ah-ō | | Raon l'Etape | rah-onh-leh-tahp′ |
| au = ō | in no | Aulne | ōwn |
| | | Auber | ō-bair′ |
| ay = ā | in ale | Aizenay | ā-z[1]-nā′ |
| | | Baraghay | bah-rah-gā′ |
| ean = ahnh | | Jean | zhahnh |
| éa = ā-ah | | St. Béas | sănh-bā-ah′ |
| eau = ō | in no | Augereau | ō-zh[1]-rō′ |
| | | Sceaux | sō |
| ei = ā | in ale | Seine | sāne |
| | | Lourdoueix | loor-doo-ā′ |
| eim ⎫ ⎬ = ăn | in anchor | | |
| ein ⎭ | | | |
| eo = o | in bore | George | zhorzh |
| éo = ā o | | Déols | dā-ol′ |
| eu = ö=i | in sir | Bayeux | bah-ee-ö′ |
| | | Argenteuil | ar-zhonh-tö′-ɣih |
| eȳ = ā | in ale | Arveyron | ar-vā-ronh′ |
| | | Ney | nā |
| ie = ee | in bee | Die | dee |
| ié = ee-eh | | Miélan | mee-ā-lanh′ |
| oa = wah | | Coarraze | kwar-rahz′ |
| | | Langoat | lahn-gwah′ |
| oe = ō-ā | | Plancoet | plahnh-cō-ā′ |
| | | Ploermel | plō-air-mel′ |

1. Commonly before *r*.   2. Commonly before *ll* followed by a vowel. In general, no rules are given by grammars for distinguishing different values of single vowel-combinations on this page.

## FRENCH—Continued.

| | | | |
|---|---|---|---|
| oi = wa | in water | Amboise | ahnh-bwoz′ |
| | | Boileau | bwaw-lō′ |
| oin = wănh | | Joinville | zhwănh-veel′ |
| | | Cysoing | see-zwănh′ |
| ou = oo | in boot | Angoulême | ahnh-goo-lāme′ |
| | | Oudinot | oo-dee-nō′ |
| oy = wa | in water | Boyer | bwaw-yā′ |
| | | Jouffroy | zhoo-frwaw′ |
| ui = wee | | Maupertuis | mō-pair-twee′ |
| | | Cuisery | kwee-zeh-ree′ |
| uy = wee | | Bruyère | brwee-yair′ |
| | | Luynes | lween |
| ch¹ = sh | | Champagne | shahm-pahñ′⁶ |
| | | Choiseul | shwoz-öl′ |
| g² = z | in leizure | Gironde | zhee-rond′ |
| | | Genlis | zhonh-lee′ |
| gl = lli | in William | Broglie | brōle-yee′ |
| gn = ni | in minion | Armagnac | ar-mahn-yahc′ |
| | | Brougniart | broon-yarr′ |
| gu = g | in get | Duguesclin | dü-guess-clănh′ |
| | | Guizot | ghee-zo′ |
| j = z | in leizure | Ajain | ah-zhănh′ |
| | | Joinville | zhwănh-veel′ |
| il³ = ee | in bee | Argenteuil | ar-zhonh-tō′-ee |
| | | Chevreul | shö-vröl′ |
| ill⁴ = y | in yes | Chantilly | shahnh-tee-yee′ |
| | | Condillac | conh-dee-yahk′ |
| qu = k | | Auquetil | ahnh-keh-teel′ |
| | | Esquirol | ess-kee-rol′ |
| s⁵ = z | | Amboise | ahm-bwoz′ |
| | | Choiseul | shwoz-öl |
| sc² = ss | | Sceaux | sso |
| | | Scey | ssā |
| th = t | | Thiers | tee-air′ |
| | | Berthollet | bair-tol-lā′ |
| w = v | | Wailly | vah-yee′ |
| | | Watteau | vah-to′ |

1. Except in names from Latin and Greek. 2. Before e, i, y.
3. Final and chiefly after vowels 4. Not initial nor before consonant.
5. Between vowels. 6. ñ = ni in minion. Of consonants between vowels, only such as may begin a word join the second of two syllables. The syllables of a French word are pronounced with nearly uniform stress, dwelling slightly, however, on the last.

## FRENCH—Continued.

| | | | |
|---|---|---|---|
| x = ks | in | Aix | ăkse |
| | | Aix-la-Chapelle | ăkse-lăh-shah-pei′ |
| | | Auxy-le-Château | ō-ksee-lö-shah-tē |
| | • | Tauxigny | to-kseen-yee′ |
| | | Zex | zheks |
| | | Paixhans | pahks-ahnh′ |
| | | Ajax | ah-zhahks′ |
| | | Alexandre | ah-leks-anh′-dr |
| x⁷ = gz | in | Xavier | gzah-vee-ă′ |
| | | Xerxes | gzair-ssess′ |
| x = ss | in | Aix-en-Province | ace-onh-pro-vănhss′ |
| | | Auxerre | o-sair′ |
| | | Auxonne | o-sonn′ |
| | | Bruxelles | brü-ssel′ |
| x | is silent in | Bayeux | bI-yö′. |
| | | Lourdoñeix | loor-doo-ă′ |
| | | Sceaux | sō |
| z = ss | in | Metz | metss |
| | | Suez | su-ess′ |

7. Initial and after initial *e*.

# ITALIAN.

| | | | |
|---|---|---|---|
| a = a | in ah | Amalfi | ah-mahl'-fee |
| | | Caracci ´ | kah-raht'-chee |
| e = ā | in ale | Veglia | văle'-yah |
| | | Alfieri | ahl-fee-ā'-ree |
| i = ee | in bee | Piombini | pee-om-bee'-nee |
| | | Bianchini | bee-ahn-kee'-nee |
| u = oo | in boot | Abruzzo | ah-broot'-so |
| | | Castrucci | cahss-troot'-chee |
| c[1] = tch | | Piacenza | pee-ah-tchent'-sah |
| | | Cellini | tchel lee'-nee |
| cc[1] = tch | | Ajaccio . | ah-yaht'-cho |
| | | Vespucci | vess-poot'-chee |
| ch = k | | Peschiera | pess-kee-ē'-rah |
| | | Cherubini | kā-roo-bee'-nee |
| gg[1] = dge | in badge | Maggiore | mah-jor'-reh |
| | | Coreggio | kor-red'-gee-o |
| gh = g | in get | Alighieri | ah-lee-ghee-ā'-ree |
| | | Borghese | bor-gā'-zeh |
| gli = lli | in million | Garigliano | gah reel-yah'-no |
| | | Cagliostro | kahl-yee os'-tro |
| gn = ñi | in minion | Campagna | kahm-pahn'-yah |
| | | Carmagnola | kahr-mahn-yō'-lah |
| j = ee | in bee | Jomelli | ee-o-mel'-lee |
| | | Brescia | bresh'-shee-ah |
| sc = sh | | Scioppius | shee-op'-pee-ooss |
| sch = sk | | Peschiera | pess-kee-ā'-rah |
| | | Brunelleschi | broo-nel-les'-kee |
| z = ds | | Zampieri | dsahm-pee-ā'-ree |
| z = ts | | Lanzi | lahnt'-see |

1. Before *e* and *i*. Two or more vowels together, each as if single. Double consonants doubly distinct. Whole enunciation round and full.

# GERMAN.

| | | | |
|---|---|---|---|
| a = a | in ah | Ranke | rahn'-keh |
| | | Hartmann | hart'-mahn |
| e = e | in eh | Menzel | men'-tsel |
| | | Mendelssohn | men'-dels-zohn |
| i = ee | in bee | Ideler | ee'-deh-ler |
| | | Ihne | ee'-neh |
| i = ĭ | in pin | Zillerthal | tsil'-ler-tahl |
| | | Rothschild | rōt'-shilt |
| u¹ = oo | in boot | Usedom | oo'-zeh-dom |
| | | Uhland | oo'-lant |
| u² = oo | in book | Adelung | ah'-deh-loong |
| | | Humboldt | hoom'-bolt |
| u³ = ü | | Saarbrück | sahr'-brück |
| | | Rückert | rü'-kert |
| y = ee | in bee | Lychen | lee'-ch-hen |
| aa = a | in ah | Aargau | ahr'-gŏw |
| | | Waagen | vah'-ghen |
| ae = ä = ae | in Gael | Laer (Lär) | laer (nearly lair) |
| | | Maeddler (Mäddler) | maed'-ler |
| ai = ī | in pine | Behaim | beh'-hīme |
| | | Mittermaier | mit'-ter-mī er |
| au = ŏw | in cow | Zwikkau | tsvik'-kŏw |
| | | Auerbach | ŏw'-er-bach-h |
| ay = ī | in pine | Thaya | tī'-ah |
| | | Mayer | mī'-er |
| ee = ā | in ale | Beethoven | bā'-tō-ven |
| | | Heeren | hā'-ren |
| ei = ī | in pine | Eisenach | ī'-zen-ach-h |
| | | Reichenbach | rī'- ch-hen-bach-h |
| eo = eh-ŏ | | Leonhard | leh'-ŏn-hart |
| | | Georg | gheh-orgh' |
| eu = oi | | Eupen | oi'-pen |
| | | Leutze | loit'-seh |
| ey = ī | in pine | Seybusch | zī'-boosh |
| | | Heyse | hī'-seh |
| ie = ee | in bee | Wien | veen |
| | | Tieck | teek |
| oe = ö = i | in sir | Goethe (Göthe) | gö'-teh |
| | | Froebel | frö'-bel |
| oo = ō | in no | Langeroog | lahng'-er-ōgh |
| ou = oo | in boot | Bouterwek | boo'-ter-vek |
| | | Houwald | hoo'-valt |

1. At the end of a syllable or before an *h* in the same syllable.
2. Except as in 1. 3. To produce this sound, let the learner, while uttering and without interrupting a broad *uh*, attempt to whistle. Accent in general on first syllable.

## GERMAN—Continued.

| | | | |
|---|---|---|---|
| $b^1 = p$ | | Taubmann | tŏwp'-mahn |
| | | Lübke | lüp'-keh |
| $c^2 = ts$ | | Decius | dā'-tsee-oos |
| | | Salice | sah-leet'-seh |
| $d^1 = t$ | | Friedland | freed'-lant |
| | | Uhland | oo'-lant |
| $g^3 = zh$ | | Angely | ahn'-zheh-lee |
| | | Genée | zhŏ-nā' |
| $g^4 = gh$ | | Schlegel | shlegh'-el |
| | | Sontag | son'-tagh |
| $g^5 = g$ | in get | Giessen | gees'-sen |
| | | Poggendorf | pogg'-en-dorf |
| $j = y$ | | Johannes | yo-han'-nase |
| | | Jacobi | yah-cŏ'-by |
| $qu = kv$ | | Quelle | kvel'-leh |
| | | Quirinus | kvee-ree'-noos |
| $v^6 = f$ | | Voss | foss |
| | | Vogelweide | fo'-ghel-vī'-deh |
| $v^7 = v$ | | Venedig | veh'-neh-digh |
| | | Beethoven | ba'-tŏ-ven |
| $w^8 = v$ | | Wien | veen |
| | | Schwartzenberg | shvarts'-en-bergh |
| $z = ts$ | | Zurich | tsoo'-rich-h |
| | | Zumpt | tsoompt |
| $ch^9 = ch\text{-}h$ | | Giessbach | gees'-bach-h |
| | | Fichte | fich'-h teh |
| $sch = sh$ | | Schönbrunn | shön'-broon |
| | | Scheffer | shef'-fer |
| $th = t$ | | Barth | bart |
| | | Thalberg | tahl'-berg |
| $zsch = tsh$ | | Zschoppen | tshŏp'-pen |
| | | Zschokke | tshok'-keh |

1. b and d, final or before any consonant except b, d, l, and r, = p and t respectively. 2. Before ä, e, i, and y. 3. In names borrowed from the French. This sound is that of z in *leizure*. 4. When final or before any consonant except g, l. n. r. 5. Except as in 3 and 4. 6. Except as in 7. 7. In the middle of words before a vowel and in foreign words. 8. Not a full v, but a combination of w and v. 9. Not a palatal, but a guttural sound, most easily pronounced by a beginner after a broad *ah*. The position of the vocal organs is then very literally the same as in the act of "gargling" the throat. From this broad "*ach!*" the learner may proceed by degrees to narrower and narrower vowel sounds, placed at first before, then both before and after, and at last only after the *ch*. In names taken from the French, *ch* retains its French sound of *sh*.

# SPANISH.

| | | | |
|---|---|---|---|
| a = a | in ah | Cartagena | car-tah-ha'-nah |
| | | Narvaez | nahr-vah'-āthe |
| e¹ = ā | in ale | Leon | lā'-on |
| | | Rebolledo | rā-bol-yā'-tho |
| e² = e | in eh | Alicante | ah-lee-cahn'-tch |
| | | Theodisele | tā-o-dee'-sch-lch |
| i = ee | in bee | Lerida | lā-ree'-thah⁵ |
| | | Ramiro | rah-mee'-ro |
| u = oo | | Murcia | moor'-thee⁴-a |
| | | Supelveda | sā-pool'-vā-tha |
| | | | |
| ae = ah-ā | | Baena | bah-ā'-nah |
| | | Paez | pah-āthe |
| ai = I | | Concentaina | con-thāne⁴-tI'-nah |
| ay = I | | Jayme | hah'-ee-meh |
| ei = ā | | Almeira | ahl-mā'-ee-rah |
| | | Ribeiro | ree-bā'-ee-ro |
| eu = ā-oo | | Teulada | tā-oo-lah'-thah⁵ |
| | | Eugenio | ā-oo-hā'-nee-o |
| ey = ā-ee | | Aspeytia | ash-pā'-ee-tee ah |
| | | Almeyda | ahl-mā'-ee-thah⁵ |
| | | | |
| b³ = v | | Excobar | ace-ee-vahr' |
| c⁴ = th | in thin | Placencia | plah-thāne⁴-thee⁴-ah |
| | | Cespedes | thāse'-pā-thāse⁵ |
| d⁵ = th | in the | Toledo | to-lā'-tho⁵ |
| | | Oviedo | o-vee-ā'-tho⁵ |
| g = h | | Gijon | hee-hon' |
| | | Clavigero | clah-vee'-hā-ro |
| gu⁶ = g | in get | Guelago | gā-lah'-go |
| | | Rodriguez | rōd-ree'-gathe |

## SPANISH—Continued.

| | | |
|---|---|---|
| h   is silent | Hojeda | o-hä'-thah[5] |
| j = h | Jaraicejo | hah-rī-tha'[4]-ho |
| | Jovellanos | ho-väle-yah'-nōce |
| lh = lli | in William Ameilhon | ah-mäle-yon' |
| ll = l:i | in William Chinchilla | cheen-cheel'-yah |
| | Murillo | moo-reel'-yo |
| ñ = ni | in minion Peñas | päne-yas' |
| | Zuniga | thoon-yee'gah |
| qu = k | Guadalquivir | gwah-dahl-kee-veer' |
| | Quevedo | kä-vä'-tho[5] |
| x = | Iznaxar | eeth-nah-har' |
| | Ximenez | hee-mä'-näth[4] |
| z = th | in thin Azaughal | ah-thow[4]-gahl' |
| | Melendez | mä-läne'-deth[4] |

1. Except as in 2.  2. Final or unaccented.  3. Between two vowels.
4. Before *e* and *i*.  5. Final or between vowels.  6. Before *a* and *o* = *gw*.  Two or more vowels together retain each its proper sound.
Accent on last syllable of words ending in a consonant, in others on the penult, unless differently marked.

# PORTUGUESE.

| | | | |
|---|---|---|---|
| a = a | in ah | Andrada | ahn-drah'-dah |
| | | Balthazar | bahl-tah'-zahr |
| e¹ = ā | in ale | Pequeno | peh-kā'-no |
| | | Pedro | pā'-dro |
| e² = ĕ | in eh | Espichel | ehs-pec-shehl' |
| | | Rezende | rēh-zehn'-deh |
| i = ee | in bee | Midoes | mee-do'-esh |
| | | Diaz | dee'-ass |
| u = oo | in boot | Funchal | foon'-shahl |
| | | Munoz | moo'-noce |
| ae = ah-eh | | Quelpaert | kehl-pah-ehrt' |
| | | Moraes | mo-rah'-esh |
| ai = I | | Favaios | fah-vāh-ee-osh |
| | | Paiva | pah'-ee-vah |
| ao = ah-ŏ | | Monçao | mon-sah'-ŏ |
| | | Joao | zho³-ah'-ŏ |
| au = ah-oo | | Araujo | ah-rah'-oo-zho |
| | | Nicolau | nee-co-lah'-oo |
| ay = I | | Fayal | fāh-ee-ahl' |
| | | Atayde | ah-tah'-ee-deh |
| ea = ā-ah | | Gouvea | goi-vā'-ah |
| | | Correa | cor-rā'-ah |
| ei = ā-ee | | Ferreira | feh-rā'-ee-rah |
| | | Ribeiro | ree-bā'-ee-ro |
| eo = ā-ŏ | | Ilheos | eel-yā'-ŏsh |
| | | Leonardo | leh-ŏ-nar'-do |
| eu = ā-oo | | Viseu | vee-sā'-oo |
| | | Abreu | ah-brā'-oo |
| ie = ee-ā | | Figaniere | fee-gah-nee-ā' reh |
| | | Viegas | vee-ā'-gahsh |
| iu = ee-oo | | Piunhi | pee-oon-yee' |

1. Ending an accented syllable. 2. Except as in 1. 3. zh = z in *leizure*. Unaccented e interchanged with *i*, unaccented *o* interchanged with *u*. Final *a. e. o*, slurred and obscure. Two or more vowels together retain each its separate sound.

## PORTUGUESE—Continued.

| | | | |
|---|---|---|---|
| oa = o-ah | | Soares | sŏ-ah'-resh |
| | | Joaquin | zhŏ''³-ah-keen |
| oe = ŏ-ch | | Goes | gŏ-esh |
| | | Midoes | mee-do'-esh |
| ou = oi | | Lourosa | loi-rŏ'-sa |
| | | Souza | soi'-zah |
| ua = oo-ah | | Duarte | doo-ar'-teh |
| | | Romualdo | ro-moo-ahl'-do |
| ue = oo-a | | Manuel | mah'-noo-ehl |
| | | | |
| ç = ss | | Guaçu | gwah-soo' |
| | | Conceição | con·sã·ee-sah'-o |
| ch = sh | | Peniche | pã-nee'-sheh |
| | | Machado | mah-shah'-do |
| g¹ = zh | | Gerez | zha'-ress |
| | | Gil | zheel |
| gu¹ = g | in get | Rodriguez | rŏ-dree'-guess |
| | | Figueira | fee-gã-ee'-rah |
| gu² = gw | | Guaçu | gwah-soo' |
| | | Guarda | gwar'-dah |
| h is silent | | Bahia | bah-ee'-ah |
| | | Hermiguez | air-mee'-guess |
| j = zh | | Jermillo | zhair-meel'-lŏ |
| | | João | zhŏ-ah'-ŏ |
| lh = lli | in million | Magalhaens | mah-gahl yah'-ensh |
| | | Coelho | cŏ-el'-yo |
| nh = ni | in minion | Minho | meen'-yŏ |
| | | Caminha | cah-meen'-yah |
| qu = k | | Pequeno | pã-kã'-no |
| | | Albuquerque | ahl-boo-kair'-keh |
| s = sh | | Goes | go'-esh |
| | | Oeiras | ŏ-ã-ee'-rash |
| th = t | | Thomaz | tŏ'-mass |
| | | Mathias | mah-tee'-ash |
| x = sh | | Azambuxeira | ah-sahm-boo-sha'-ee-rah |
| | | Xavier | shah'-vee-ehr |
| z = ss | | Portuguez | por-too-guess' |
| | | Rodriguez | ro-dree'-guess' |

1. Before *e*, *i*, *y*, = *zh* = *z* in *leizure*.  2. Before *a* and *o*.  A vowel before *m* or *n* in the same syllable is nasal.  Final *ão* is nasal. Accent on final *em*, *im*, *om*, *um*, on syllable marked with either ' or ~, and on penult of words ending in a vowel.

# DANISH.

| | | | |
|---|---|---|---|
| a = a | in ah | Skager | skah-her |
| | | Valdemar | vahl-deh-nahr |
| aa = aw | in awe | Aaröe | aw-rö'-eh |
| | | Aagaard | awl-gawrd |
| ae = e | eh | Aeröe | eh-rö'-eh |
| | | Saebygaard | seh'-bee-gawrd |
| au = ŏw | in cow | Lauridsen | lŏw'-rid-sen |
| | | Hauge | how'-heh |
| e = eh | | Egebyerg | eh'-yeh byergh[3] |
| | | Stege | steh'-yeh |
| ee = ã | in ale | Sneehaettan | snã'-hettan |
| | | Skeel | skäle |
| ei = ī | in pine | Eightved | ight'-vehd |
| | | Heiberg | hī'-berg |
| eu = ö = i | in sir | Geuss | göss |
| | | Deurs | dörss |
| ej = ī | in pine | Ejdsvold | īds'-vold |
| | | Vejlby | vīle'-bee |
| ey = ī | in pine | Feye | fī'-yeh |
| | | Beyer | bī'-yer |
| i = ee | in bee | Fibiger | fee'-bee-her |
| | | Blicher | blee'-ch-her[2] |
| ie = ee-eh | | Spieröe | spee-eh-rö'-eh |
| | | Bielke | bee-el'-keh |
| ii = ee | in bee | Germiin | yer'-meen |
| | | Friis | frees |
| ö = ö = i | in sir | Sören | sö'-ren |
| | | Malmö | mahl'-mö |
| öe = ö-eh | | Färöe | feh-rö'-eh |
| | | Bergsöe | bergh-sö-eh |
| öj = ö-ee | | Vemmehöj | vehm'-meh-hö-ee |
| | | Vöjen | vö'-ee-en |
| u = oo | in book | Ulkerup | ool'-keh-roop |
| | | Ulrik | ool'-reek |
| ü¹ = ü | | Jürgensen | yür'-hen-sen |
| | | Fürsen | für'-sen |
| ue = oo-eh | | Huenicken | hoo-eh' nee-ken |
| ui = oo-ee | | Huitfeldt-Kaas | hoo-eet' felt kawss |

1. This sound can be most easily produced, if, while prolonging a broad *ah*, and without interrupting the sound, the learner attempt to whistle. 2. *ch-h* = an extremely rough *h*. 3. *gh* = a hard *g* slurred.

## DANISH—Continued.

| | | | |
|---|---|---|---|
| uu = oo | in boot | Aarhuus | awr'-hooce |
| | | Bruun | broon |
| y = ee | in bee | Tyge | tee'-yeh |
| | | Jyden | yee'-den |
| ch = ch-h[6] | | Jochumsen | yo'-ch-hoom-sen |
| | | Esmarch | es'-march-h |
| d[1] hardly heard | | Hvidkilde | veed'-keel-leh |
| | | Throndhjem | tronn'-yem |
| g[2] = h, i or y | | Gimsö[3] | heem'-sö |
| | | Norge | nor'-ieh |
| | | Egemark | eh'-yeh-mark |
| | | Ingeborg | een'-yeh-borh |
| g in gj silent | | Gjellerup | yel'-leh-roop |
| | | Gjemsöe | yem'-sö-eh |
| g before n = w | | Agnhammer | öwn'-ham-mer |
| | | Soguefiord | söw'-neh-fyord |
| g elsewhere hard | | Slagelse | slah'-ghel-seh |
| | | Aagaard | aw'-gawrd |
| h silent in hj | | Hjarnöe | yar'-nö-eh |
| | in hv | Hjertesorg | yehr'-tes-orgh |
| | in th | Hvide | vee'-dheh[1] |
| | | Thorsöe | tor'-sö-eh |
| | | Bardenfleth | bar'-den-flet |
| j = y = ee | | Öfjord | ö'-fyord |
| | | Jörgen | yör'-ghen |
| sk[4] before e, i, y | | Bortskjaenken | bort'-shehn-ken |
| | | Skjalm | shahlm |
| skj[4] a, o, u = sh | | Arentskjold | ah'-rent-shol |
| | | Skjöde | shö'-deh |
| sch = sh | | Schiönning | shee-ö'-ning |
| | | Schojen | shö'-yen |
| schj = shee | | Schjellerup | shee-el'-leh-roop |
| | | Schjörring | shee-ör'-ring |
| th = t | | Thorkill | tor'-kil |
| | | Günther | gün'-ter |
| v[5] = u or w | | Brunlavq | broon'-löwk |
| | | Poulsker | pöwl'-sker |
| w = v | | Drewsen | drev'-sen |
| | | Erslew | er'-slev |

1. Between vowels and after *l*, *n*, *r* or *t*. 2. Before *a*, *e*, *i*, *ö*, *y*, in the same syllable. 3. *ö* = *i* in *sir*. 4. In Norway. 5. Before any consonant before which *v* cannot easily retain its proper sound, as in *Kjöbenhavn* = *kyö-ben-hown*. 6. An extremely rough *h*. In Scandinavia, even more than elsewhere, is felt the want of any settled standard of spelling and pronunciation. In Danish, as in other languages in this hand-book, the aim has been so to choose between varying forms, as to give least difficulty to an English-speaking person.

# DUTCH.

On this page more than the average deficiencies of the grammars had to be supplemented, and the compiler bespeaks corresponding indulgence.

| | | | |
|---|---|---|---|
| a = a | in ah | Amsterdam | ahm'-stair-dahm |
| | | Te Water | tā-vah'-ter |
| aa = a | in ah | Aalsmeer | ahls'-māre |
| | | Boerhaave | boor'-hah-veh |
| ae = a | in ah | Aertrycke | ahr'-trī-keh |
| | | Spaendonck | spahn'-donck |
| ai = I | in pine | Lairesse | lī rās'-seh |
| | | Aitzema | ite-za'-mah |
| au = ŏw | | Nassau | nahs'-sow |
| | | Gaubius | hou'-bee-ces |
| e = ā | in ale | Zele | zā'-lā |
| | | Elzevir | ale'-zā-veer |
| ee = ā | in ale | Aalanderveen | ah'-lahn-dair-vane |
| | | Heemskirk | hames'-keerk |
| ei = I | in pine | Reiz | rīz |
| | | Beijerland | bi'-air-lant |
| eu = ŏ = i | in bird | Deurhoff | dör-hof |
| | | Wijk-bej-Heusden | vike'-bi-höss'-den |
| i = ee | in bee | Brill | breel |
| | | Limborch | leem'-borch-h |
| ie = ee | in bee | Biesbosch | bees-bosk' |
| | | Diemerbrock | deem'-air-brok |
| y = I | in pine | Baardwijk | bahrd'-vike |
| | | Joncktijs | yonk'-tice |
| oe = oo | in boot | Broek | brook |
| | | Binkershoek | been'-kair shook |
| oo = ŏ | in bone | Groot | grote |
| | | Noordwijkerhout | nort'-vi-kair-howt |
| ou = ŏw | in cow | Abcoude | ahb'-kow-deh |
| | | Oudendorp | ow'-den-dorp |
| u = ee | in bee | Ruhnken | reen'-ken |
| | | Utrecht | ee'-trech-ht |
| uu = ee | in bee | Duur-stede | deer'-stā deh |
| ui = oi | in oil | Buitensluis | boit'-en-slois |
| | | Hemsterhuis | hame'-ster-hoiss |
| aai = ah-ee | | Maaijen | mah'-ee-yen |
| aau = ŏw | in cow | Blaauw | blah-ow |

## DUTCH—Continued.

| | | | |
|---|---|---|---|
| ceu = ö | | Leeuwenhoek | lö'-ven-hook |
| ieu = ee-yu | | Nieuwport | nee-yu-port |
| oei = oo-ee | | Goeije | hoo'-ee-yeh |
| ooi = o-ee | | Hooijer | ho'-ee-yer |
| y = I | | Mytens | mI'-tens |
| uy = oi | in oil | Muylwijk | moil'-vike |
| ch¹ = ch-h | | Maestricht | mahs'-trich-ht |
| | | Limborch | leem'-borch-h |
| d³ = t | | Vlieland | vlee'-lant |
| | | Gerard | hä'-rart |
| g³ = h | | Gouda | höw'-dah |
| | | Gerard | hä-rart' |
| g⁴ = gh-h | | Baelegem | bah'-leh-gh-hem |
| | | Hoog | högh-h |
| s = ss | | Goes | hooss |
| | | Wauvermans | wöw'-ver-manss |
| sch = sk | | Bies-Bosch | beess-bosk' |
| | | Schrevelius | skrä-vä'-lee-ees |
| th = t | | Nethen | nä'-tane |
| | | Both | bôte |
| w⁵ = v | | Wijk | vIke |
| | | Wyttenbach | vI'-ten-bach-h |
| w² is silent | | Wouw | vöw |
| | | Blaauw | blah'-öw |

1. An aspirate guttural, most easily pronounced after a broad *ah*.
2. When final. 3. When initial. 4. When not initial. This sound is a hard *g* slurred. 5. When not final. Accent in general on the first radical syllable.

# SWEDISH.

| | | | |
|---|---|---|---|
| a = a | in ah | Dalaröch | dah-lah-rö'-eh |
| | | Akerblad | ah'-ker-blahd |
| ä = ä | in a'e | Hälleström | hehl'-es-tröm |
| | | Forshäll | for'-shäle |
| aa = å = aw | in awe | Haartman | hawrt'-mahn |
| | | Haastesko | haws-tes'-ko |
| ae = ä | in ale | Maelar | mä'-lahr |
| | | Linnaeus | lin-nä'-oos |
| au = ŏw | in cow | Brauner | brŏw'-ner |
| | | Paul | pŏwl |
| e = e | in eh | Ranea | rah'-neh-ah |
| | | Bremer | breh'-mer |
| ee = ä | in ale | Hylteen | yeel'-tane |
| i¹ = ee | in bee | Nikander | nee-kahn'-der |
| | | Ihre | ee'-reh |
| eu = ö = i | in sir | Heurlin | hör'-lin |
| | | Jedeur | yeh'-dör |
| o² = oo | in book | Olaus | oo-lah'-oos |
| | | Olof | oo'-lof |
| ö = i | in sir | Faeglöe | fä-glö'-eh |
| | | Grönvall | grön'-vall |
| oo = ō | | Gyllenkrook | yeel'-en-krōke |
| | | Grooth | grōte |
| u = oo | in book | Upsala | oop-sah'-lah |
| | | Humerus | hoo'-meh-roos |
| ü = ü | | Hülphers | hül'-fers |
| uu = oo | in boot | Juusten | yoos'-ten |
| y = ee | in bee | Gyllenborg | yeel'-en-borh |
| | | Byström | bee'-ström |

1. Ending syllable or before *h* in same syllable.  2. Ending syllable

## SWEDISH—Continued.

| | | |
|---|---|---|
| bj = bee | Björkman | byörk'-mahn |
| | Bjelke | byel'-keh |
| ch³ = ch    in chair | Chenon | cheh'-non |
| ch⁴ = k | Christina | kriss-tee'-nah |
| | Echman | ek'-mahn |
| d⁵    is silent | Djurberg | yoor'-berh |
| f⁶ = v | Gefle | yev'-leh |
| | Gustaf | goos'-tav |
| fv⁷ | Harfvefeldt | har'-veh felt |
| | Hofverberg | hov'-ver-berh |
| g⁸ = h | Djurberg | yoor'-berh |
| g⁹ = y | Gyllenborg | yeel'-en borh |
| gj = y | Gjädda | yehd'-bah |
| gn = ngn | Tegner | teng'-ner |
| g = g    in get | Gustaf | goos'-tav |
| j = y | Johan | yo'-hahn |
| | Jordanus | yor'-dah-noos |
| qv = kv | Hernquist | hern'-kvist |
| sk⁹ = sh | Eksjo | ek'-shö |
| sj, skj, stj, tj = sh | Bjornstjerne | byörn'-sher-neh |
| th = t | Frithiof | frit'-yov |

3. Initial except in *chr*.   4. Except as in 3.   5. Before *j* and *t*.
6. Ending syllable.   7. In simple word *fv* = *v;* in compound = *vu.*
8. Final after *l* or *r*.   9. Before *e, i, y, ä, ö*.   Accent in general on first syllable.

# HUNGARIAN.

| | | | |
|---|---|---|---|
| á = a | in ah | Jász-Berény | yahss'-bā-reñ' [b] |
| | | Deák | dā-ahk' |
| aa = a | in ah | Kezd-Szaaz | kezd'-sahz |
| a = aw | in awe | Baja | baw'-yaw |
| | | Aba | aw'-baw |
| e = e | in eh | Debreczin | deh-bret'-sin |
| | | Sellye | sel'-yeh |
| i = ee | in bee | Iloncza | ee-lon'-tsaw |
| | | Tisza | tee'-saw |
| ö = ɔ = i | in sir | Böszörmény | bö-sör-mehñ' |
| | | Görgey | gör-ghI |
| u = oo | in boot | Buda | boo'-daw |
| | | Kossuth | kosh-shoot' |
| ü = ee | in bee | Füzes | fee'-zesh |
| | | Güns | gheensh |
| y = ee[1] | in bee | Zagyva | zaw-zhee'-vaw |
| | | | |
| ai = I | in pine | Baimocz | bI'-mots |
| ay = oi | | Tokay | to-koi |
| ei = I | in pine | Lei-tha | lI'-tah |
| | | Geib | ghIbe |
| eö = ö = i | in sir | Eötvös | öt-vösh |
| | | Beöthy | bö-tee |
| eu = oi | in oil | Leuka | loi'-kaw |
| ew = ö = i | in sir | Tö-rök | thewrewk |
| ey = I | in pine | Leygen | lI'ghen |

## HUNGARIAN—Continued.

| | | | |
|---|---|---|---|
| g = j[2] | | Gyorgy | jörj |
| | | Nyiregyháza | ñee-rej-hah'-zaw |
| g = zh[3] | | Zagyva | zaw-zhee'-vaw |
| g = g[4] | in get | Görgey | gör-ghI |
| | | Geib | ghibe |
| j = y = ee | | Rajecz | rah-ee-ets' |
| | | Uj Var | oo-ee-vawr' |
| s = sh | | Selmécz | shel-mets' |
| | | Satoralja | shah-to-rawl'-yaw |
| cs = ch | | Csaba | chaw'-baw |
| | | Rácz | r-rahts |
| cz = ts | | Teplicz | tep-leets |
| | | Czuszor | tsoo-tsorr |
| sz = ss | | Szegedin | sseh-gheh-deen' |
| | | Széchényj | sseh-chehn'-yee |
| th = t | | Theisz | tice |
| | | Majthenyj | mi-tehn'-yee |
| zs = zh | | Kovezsd | ko'-vezhd |
| | | Dozsa | do'-zhaw |
| ly = lli | in William | Mihály | mee-haI' |
| ny = ni | in minion | Batthyány | baht-yahñ'[5] |

No rule is given to take the place of the written accent in distinguishing the two sounds of á and a.

1. Except as silent in 2. 2. Before y or hy, either final, or followed by a vowel, or by h and a vowel. 3. Before y forming a syllable. This sound is that of z in leizure. 4. Except as in 2 and 3. 5. ñ = ni in minion.

# RUSSIAN.

| a = a | in ah | Tarasska | tah-rahss'-kah |
| | | Derjavine | der-zhah'-⁵veen |
| ä = e · | in eh | Wjäsemsky | vee-eh-sem'-skee |
| e = e | in eh | Turgenjew | toor-gehn'-yef |
| i = ee | in bee | Kniajnine | knee-azh'⁵-neen |
| | | Bilibine | bee-lee-been |
| u = oo | in boot | Puschkin | poosh'-keen |
| | | Iurij | ee-oo'-ree |
| y = ee | in bee | Davydow | dah-vee'-dof |
| | | Lyof | lee'-off |
| | | | |
| ai = I | in pine | Yasnaia | yahss-nI'-ah |
| | | Vagai | vah ghI |
| ay = I | in pine | Maykof | mI-koff |
| | | Kayva | kI-vah |
| ei = eh-ee | | Heinenn | heh-ee-nen |
| | | Seim | seh-eem |
| ej = eh-ee | | Voronej | vo-ro-neh'ee |
| ej = ezh | | Nadejda | nah'-dezh⁵-dah |
| ie = ee-eh | | Griboiedoff | gree-bo-ee-eh'-doff |
| | | Dniepr | d'nee-ehp'-r |
| ij = ee | | Dmitrijeff | d'mee'-tree-ef |
| | | Jurij | ee-oo'-ree |
| oi = oy | in boy | Tolstoi | tol'-stoy |
| | | Polevoi | po-leh-voy' |
| ou = oo | in boot | Godounof | go-doo'-noff |
| | | Koutouzof | koo-too'-zoff |
| | | Bestouchef | bes-too'-shef |

## RUSSIAN—Continued.

| | | |
|---|---|---|
| ch = sh | Pouchkine | poosh'-keen |
| ch = tch | Karamych | kah-rah-meetch' |
| ch = ch-h[1] | Choczim | ch-ho-tcheem' |
| | Chmelnizkj | ch-hmel-neets'-ky |
| cz = tch | Choczim | ch-ho-tcheem' |
| g = g    in get | Jelagine | ych-lah-gheen' |
| j = ee = y | Wjatka | vee-aht'-kah |
| | Andrej | ahn-dreh-ee |
| | | |
| j = zh[6] | Joukovsky | zhoo-kov'-ski |
| | Nijni | neezh'[5]-nee |
| kh = ch-h[1] | Khomiakof | ch-ho-mee-ah'-koff |
| sch = sh | Daschkow | dahsh'-koff |
| tsch = tch | Tschernytschew | tcher-nee-tchef' |
| | Tatischtschew | tah-teesh-tchef' |
| w = v = f[2] | Kiew | kee-ef' |
| | Lermontow | ler'-mon-toff |
| | Lomonozow | lom-o-no'-zoff |
| | Krylow | kree'-loff |
| z = z[3] | Karamzin | kah-rahm-zeen' |
| z = ts[4] | Herzen | hert'-sen |
| | Rjumanzow | ree-oo-mahut's-off |

1. A guttural sound, an extremely rough *h*. 2. *w*, *v*, and *j* are used as respectively German, French, and English equivalents for the same Russian letter, but are interchanged without rule or consistency. 3. French and English. 4. German. 5. *zh = z* in *leizure*. 6. The French equivalent.

# POLISH.

| | | | |
|---|---|---|---|
| a = a | in ah | Warszawa | var-shah'-vah |
| | | Lubawa | loo bah'-vah |
| c = c | in ch | Kamieniec | kahm-yen'-yets |
| | | Brzesc · | bzhests |
| i = ee | in bee | Kazimirz | kah'-zee meerzh |
| | | Swinka | sveen'-kah |
| u = oo | in book | Pultusk | pool'-toosk |
| | | Bruc | broots |
| y = ee | in bee | Kryytyn | kree-ee'-teen |
| | | Hryczyna | hree-tchee'-nah |
| aj = I | in pine | Eiecjuajtis | I-tsee nI'-teess |
| | | Beloszajtis | beh-lo-shI'-teess |
| au = ŏw | in cow | Gaudowicz | gŏw'-do-veetch |
| | | Kamblau | kahm'-blŏw |
| ay = I | in pine | Wyzayny | vee-zI' nee |
| | | Gwiazay | gvee-ah-zI |
| ej = I | in pine | Biejkŏwski | bee-I kof'-skee |
| | | Bejnar | bI'-nar |
| ey = I | in pine | Boreyko | bo-rI'-ko |
| | | Bieykŏwski | bee-I-kof'-skee |
| ie = ee eh | | Mieszkow | mee-esh'-kov |
| oj = oy | in boy | Bojanek | bo-yah' nek |
| | | Girdwoju | geerd'-voyn |
| ou = oo | in boot | Prokourov | pro-koo'-rov |

# POLISH—Continued.

| | | | |
|---|---|---|---|
| c = ts | | Makowiec | mah-ko'-vee-ets |
| | | Mococ | mō'-tsots |
| g = g | in get | Grzegorzew | gzhch-gor'-zhev |
| | | Boygis | boy'-gheess |
| j = y | | Jalpushkov | yahl-poosh'-kov |
| | | Kujawach | koo-yah-vach-h |
| w = v | | Wawrzenczyci | vahv-zhen-tchest'-see |
| | | Wladislawow | vlah-dis-lah'-vov |
| | | | |
| ch = ch h | | Socharczew | so-ch-har'-chev |
| | | Borch | borch-h |
| cz = tch | | Buczacz | bootch'-ahtch |
| | | Bodziewicz | bo-jee-ch-vitch |
| dz = j | | Dzialoszice | jee-ah-lo-sheet'-seh |
| | | Dziwidzinski | jee-vee-jeen'-skee |
| rz = zh | | Brzesc | bzhests' |
| sz = sh | | Szymanowski | shee-mah-nof'-skee |
| | | Szeszuppe | shch-shoo'-peh |
| szcz = sh-tch | | Szczuzin | shtchoo'-zeen |
| | | Goszczyza | gosh-tcheet'-zah |

Accent in general on penult. In difficult combinations of consonants insert obscure e; e. g., in Krzczecki, k(e)rzh-tchets'-kee; Gwozdʹ,
g(e)vozh j(e); Wezele, (e)v-tcheh'-leh.

# BOHEMIAN.

| | | | |
|---|---|---|---|
| a = ah | in ah | Mazakova | mah-zhah-ko'-vah |
| | | Czaslau | chass'-low |
| e = e | in eh | Swetla | svet'-lah |
| i = ee | in bee | Bilin | bee-leen' |
| | | Bidschow | beet'-shov |
| u = oo | in boot | Chlumecz | ch-hloo'-mets |
| | | Swatopluk | svato-plook |
| y = ee | in bee | Mokry | mo'-kree |
| au = ŏw | in cow | Lischau | lee'-shŏw |
| | | Auscha | ŏw'-shah |
| ie = ee | in bee | Mies | mees |
| ie = ee-eh | | Wognomiestetz | vog-no-mee-es-tets |
| ou = oo | in boot | Kalousek | kah loo-sek |
| c = ts¹ | | Cernowitz | tser'-no-veets |
| c = tch | | Studnicka | stood-neetch'-kah |
| g = g | in get | Eger | eh'-gher |
| j = y | | Jaromirz | yah'-ro-meerts |
| | | Jirasek | yee'-rah-sek |
| w = v | | Wlaschim | vlah'-sheem |
| | | Wscherau | vsheh'-rŏw |
| z = ts¹ | | Zasmuk | tsahs'-mook |
| | | Zizelitz | tsee'-tsch-leets |
| z = zh | | Mazakova | mah-zhah-ko vah |
| | | Bozena | bo-sheh'-nah |
| ch = ch-h² | | Chocholousek | ch-ho-ch-ho-loo-sek |
| | | Hainspuch | hine'-spooch |
| cz = ts | | Sczemecz | sch'-tsch-mets |
| rz = zh | | Brzesnice | bzhes'-neet-sch |
| | | Przischowitz | pzhee'-sho-veets |

Accent in general on first syllable. In difficult combinations of consonants insert obscure e; e. g., mlceti, m(e)l-tcheh-tee; mrznouti, m(e)rzh-noo-tee. 1. No rule is given for distinguishing between the two sounds of c and the two of z in the absence of the written accent. 2. ch-h = an extremely rough h.

# SERVIAN.

| | | | |
|---|---|---|---|
| a = a | in ah | Slatina | slah-tee′-nah |
| | | Parachin | pah-rah-cheen′ |
| e = e | in eh | Jephrem | yef′-rehm |
| | | Deligrad | deh′-lee-grahd |
| i = ee | in bee | Brianie | bree-ah′-nee eh |
| | | Diunis | dee-oo-nees |
| u = oo | | Kurshumli | koor-shoom-lee |
| | | Ultschin | oolt-sheen |
| ai = I | | Maidanpek | mi-dahn-pek |
| ou = oo | | Csookour | tchoo-koor |
| | | | |
| c = ts | | Cernojewitsch | tser-no-yeh veetch |
| | | Siljegovac | seel-yeh-go-vahts |
| g = g | in get | Jagodina | yah-go-dee′-na |
| | | Margareta | mar-gah-reh′-tah |
| ch = tch | | Chupria | tchoo′-pree-ah |
| | | Parachin | pah-rah-cheen′ |
| cs = tch | | Csoukour | tchoo-koor |
| | | Nikcolies | nee-ko-leetch |
| dj = d′ye | | Medvedj | med-ved′ye |
| | | Stojan | sto′-yahn |
| j = y | | Kjuprija | kyoo-pree′-yah |
| lj = l′ye | | Valjevo | val-yeh′-vo |
| | | Radalj | rah-dahl′ye |
| nj² = ñ | | Njeresnitza | nyeh-res-neet′-sah |
| | | Krupanj | kroo-pahñ |
| s = ss | | Knes | kness |
| sch = sh | | Milasch | mee-lash |
| | | Nisch | neesh |
| dsch = j | | Kujundschitsch | koo-yoon-jeetch |
| tsch = tch | | Obrenowitsch | o-bren′-o-veetch |
| w = v | | Iwan | ee′-vahn |
| | | Dobrowitz | do′-bro-veets |
| x = zh¹ | | Maxim | mah-zheem′ |
| | | Alexinats | ah-leh′-zhee-nahts |

Grammars give no rule for accent that can be of service here.
1. z̧ = z in *leizure.* 2. This sound is that of *ni* in *minion.*

3

## MODERN GREEK.

| | | | |
|---|---|---|---|
| a = a | in ah | Patras | pah-trahss' |
| | | Ambrakia | ahm-brah'-kee-ah |
| e = e | in eh | Decelia | theh-keh' lee-ah |
| | | Spezzie | spet'-see a |
| i = ee | in bee | Dirakhi | thee-rach-h-ee |
| | | Thiaki | thee-ah-kee |
| o = aw | in awe | Domokos | thaw'-maw-kos |
| | | Marathona | mah-rah-thaw-nah |
| u = ee | in bee | Druva | three'-vah |
| | | Thuria | thee'-ree-ah |
| y = ee | in bee | Katavryta | kah-tah-vree'-tah |
| | | Hydra | hee'-thrah |
| ae = eh | in eh | Aegialeae | eh-yee-ah'-leh-eh |
| | | Mycenae | mee-keh'-neh |
| ai = e | in eh | Gaidourokhori | geh-thoo-raw-ch-haw'-ree |
| | | Xilogaidara | xee-law-geh'-dah-rah |
| au$^1$ = av | | Mauro | mav'-ro |
| | | Auliotes | av-lee-aw'-tehs |
| au$^2$ = af | | Naupacto | naf-pahk'-to |
| ei = ee | in bee | Zeitoun | zee'-toon |
| | | Cleitor | klee'-tor |
| eo = eh o | | Cleonae | kleh'-aw-neh |
| | | Neokhori | neh-aw-ch-haw'-ree |
| eu$^1$ = ev | | Euripus | ev'-ree-pees |
| eu$^2$ = ef | | Leucadia | lef-kah'-dee-ah |
| ie = ee-eh | | Kekhries | kek'-ch-hree-es |
| oi = ee | in bee | Lantzoy | lahnt'-zee |
| | | Oxoi | aw'-xee |

## MODERN GREEK—Continued.

| | | | |
|---|---|---|---|
| b = v | | Bathi | vah'-thee |
| c = k | | Caenepolis | ken-neh'-paw-lees |
| d = th | in the | Polydendri | paw-lee-then'-three |
| g³ = y | in yes | Gyaros | yee ah'-raws |
| g² = ः | in get | Golemi | gaw'-leh-mee |
| j = y | | Genidji | yeh'-nee-jee |
| kh = ch-h | | Katokhi | kah-taw'-ch-hee |
| p⁴ = b | | Olympos | aw-leem'-baws |
| s = z⁵ | | Smyrna | zmeer'-nah |
| t = d⁶ | | Lepanto | leh-pahn'-daw |
| ts = ch³ | | Tserina | cheh ree'-nah |
| tz = dz = j⁶ | | Tzintzina | jeen-jeen'-ah |

1. Before *b, d, g, l, m, n, r.*  2. Elsewhere.  3. Before *e, i, y.*
4. After *m.*  5. Before *b, d, g, m, n, r.*  6. After *n.*  Stress of voice in Modern Greek follows written accents, which are not reproduced with Roman characters, in connection with which, however, their place cannot well be supplied by written rules.

# TURKEY IN EUROPE.

| | | | |
|---|---|---|---|
| a = a | in ah | Zara | zah-rah′ |
| | | Kara Hissar | kah′-rah-his-sar′ |
| e = e | in eh | Abdera | ab deh′-rah |
| | | Yenija | yen′-ee jah |
| i = ee | in bee | Chiti | kee′-tee |
| | | Sitia | see-tee′-ah |
| | | Osmandjik | os-mahn-jeek′ |
| i = ĭ | in pin | Musjid | mus-jid′ |
| u = oo | in boot | Modurli | mo-door′-lee |
| | | Unua | oon′-nah |
| | | Scutari | scoo-tah-ree′ |
| u = ŭ | in but | Musjid | mus-jid′ |
| ü = ü | | Altüntach | ah-lün-tach-h |
| y = ĭ | in pin | Jassy | yahs′-sĭ |
| | | | |
| ai = I | | Jaicza | jĭ′-tsah |
| | | Zai | zĭ |
| au = ŏw | | Arnautkoi | ar-naut′-koi |
| ay = I | | Kavaya | kah-vĭ′-yah |
| | | Bayazid | bĭ-yah-zeed′ |
| ei = ā | | Sumaisat | soo-mā-saht′ |
| | | Hossein | hos-sāne′ |
| ey = I | | Seyyid | sĭ-yeed′ |
| ie = ee-eh | | Bielopol | bee-eh-lo′-pol |
| ou = oo | | Isoglou | ee-so-gloo′ |
| ui = wee | | Tanuirath | tahn-wee-raht′ |

## TURKEY IN EUROPE—Continued.

| | | | |
|---|---|---|---|
| ch = tch | | Chardak | tchar-dak′ |
| ch = ch-h | | Bucharest | boo-ch-hah-rest′ |
| ch = k | | Chiti | kee′-tee |
| cs = tsh | | Bihacs | bee-hahtch′ |
| cz = ts | | Jaicza | ji′-tsah |
| | | Bussovacz | boos-so-vahts′ |
| dj = j | | Osmandjik | os-man-jeek′ |
| g = g | in get | Girna | geer′-nah |
| j = j | | Sabanjah | sah-bahn′-jah |
| j = y | | Jannina | yahn′-nee-nah |
| kh = ch-h | | Bazarkhan | bah-zar-ch-hahn′ |
| th = th | | Xanthi | zahn′-thee |
| th = t | | Tanuirath | tahn-wee-raht′ |
| x = z | | Xanthi | zahn′-thee |
| zz = ts | | Gomanizza | go-mah-neet′-sah |
| dsch = j | | Dschurdschova | joor-jo′-vah |

The names on this page are not chosen as Turkish, but to serve in some measure as types of forms prevailing in Turkey, and as supplementary to the lists given as Roumanian, Servian, and Modern Greek. The same letter will represent different sounds as a name is uttered by Greek, Turk, or Slav, and it is not within the pretensions of this book to bring order out of the confusion of tongues under Turkish dominion.

# TURKEY IN ASIA.

| | | | |
|---|---|---|---|
| a = a | in ah | Kara Aghadj | kah-rah'-ah-gahj' |
| | | Kalafat | kah-lah-fah' |
| e = e | in eh | Jebel el Sheik. | jeh-behl-ehl-shɛke |
| | | Kerely | keh-reh'-lee |
| i = ee | in bee | Kerkit Chiftlik | ker-keet'-cheeft-leek' |
| | | Vezir Kopri | veh-zeer'-kō-pree' |
| u = oo | in boot | Batum | bah-toom' |
| | | Sinub | see-noob' |
| y = ee | in bee | Jebel Tyh | jeh-bel-tee' |
| | | Fyndik | feen-deek' |
| | | | |
| ae = ee | in bee | Esdreelon | ez-dree'-lon |
| ai = I | in pine | Kaisariyeh | ki-zah-ree-eh' |
| | | Ismail Bey | ees-mīle-bā |
| au = ŏw | in cow | Hauran | how-rahn' |
| | | Winaur | wee nour' |
| ay = I | in pine | Kaya Hissar | kI-yah-hees-sar' |
| ei = ā | in ale | Deir | dāre |
| | | Sumeisat | soo-mā-saht' |
| ey = ā | in ale | Beyrout | bā-root' |
| ie = ee-eh | | Dievisluk | dee-eh-veez-look' |
| ou = oo | in boot | Vourla | voor'-lah |
| | | | |
| ch = tch | | Choruk | tcho-rook' |
| | | Chandarlik | tchahn-dar-leek' |
| g = g | in get | Gind Abbas | gheend-ahb bahss' |
| | | Geira | gā'-rah |
| j = j | | Injesu | een-jeh-soo' |
| | | Guzelje | goo-zel'-jeh |

This page, like the last aims merely to give a few types of the forms prevailing within the Turkish dominions.

# ROUMANIAN.

| | | | |
|---|---|---|---|
| a = a | in ah | Bassarabia | bahs-sah-rah'-bee-ah |
| e = e | in eh | Waleni | vah-leh'-nee |
| i = ee | in bee | Kimpina | keem'-pee-nah |
| u = oo | in boot | Buchuresci | boo-koo-res'-chee |
| y = ĭ | in pin | Jassy | zhahs'-see |
| a, e, o, u = ŭ | in but | Turnu | toor'-nŭh |
| e init. = ye | | Ephraxia | yeh-phrax-ee'-ah |
| é = eh-ah | | Passeré | pahs-seh-reh'-ah |
| ó = o-ah | | Dómna | doahm'-nah |
| | | | |
| au = ou | | Bacau | bah-cŏw |
| ea = eh-ah | | Nazarettean | nah-zah-ret'-teh-ahn |
| eo = eh-o | | Buzeo | boo-zeh'-uh |
| oe = o-eh | | Ploesti | plo-es'-tee |
| ou = oo | | Cahoul | kah-ch-hool' |
| | | | |
| c = tch | | Sacieni | sah-tchee-eh'-nee |
| c = k | | Bucar | boo-kar |
| g = g | in English | Giurgevo | jee-oor-jeh'-vo |
| h = ch-h[1] | | Horezu | ch-ho-reh'-ah-zoo |
| j = zh[2] | | Crajova | krah-zho'-vah |
| š = sh | | Fokšani | fok-shah'-nee |

1 A harsh guttural sound. 2. z̆ = z in *leizure*. All final vowel-sounds slurred and obscure. No rule for accent can be given here. No rule to distinguish sounds of c or of s in absence of written accent. The acute accent over a vowel in Roumanian denotes a somewhat drawling pronunciation.

# ARABIA.

| | | | |
|---|---|---|---|
| a = a | in ah | Akabah | ah'-kah-bah |
| | | Ras-el-Had | rahss-el-hahd' |
| e = e | in eh | Kotembel | ko-tehm behl' |
| | | Beder | beh'-dehr |
| i = ee | in bee | Anizeh | ah-nee'-zeh |
| | | Perim | peh-reem' |
| u = oo | in boot | Abd-ul-Kuri | ahbd-ool-koo' ree |
| | | Suk-el-Jumakh | sook-el-joo-mach-h' |
| y = ee | in bee | Tafyle | tah-fee'-leh |
| ae = a | ✱ in ah | Graen | grahn |
| | | Taez | tahz |
| ai = I | in pine | Khaibar | ch-hI-bar' |
| | | Ain | Ine |
| au = ŏw | in cow | Hadrahmaut | hah-drah-mŏwt' |
| | | Khaulan | ch-hŏw-lahn' |
| ay = I | in pine | Tayef | tI-yef' |
| | | Ras om Haye | rahss-om-hI'-yeh |
| ei = ā | in ale | Grein | grain |
| | | Mazeira | mah-zā'-rah |
| ey = ā | in ale | El-Moeyleh | el-mō-ā'-leh |
| ie = ee-eh | | Meymounie | mā-moo'-nee-eh |
| ou = oo | in boot | Sedouan | seh-doo-ahn' |
| g = g | in get | Giadila | ghee-ah-dee'-lah |
| j = j | | Nejran | nej-rahn' |
| kh[1] = ch-h | | Akhab | ach-h-ahb' |

1. This sound is a harsh guttural.  No rule for accent.

# PERSIA, AFGHANISTAN, AND BELOOCHISTAN.

| | | | |
|---|---|---|---|
| a = a | in ah | Kandahar | kahn-dah-har′ |
| | | Hamadan | hah-mah-dahn′ |
| | | Saadi | sah′-ah-dee |
| e = e | in eh | Teheran | tah-heh-rahn′ |
| | | Deregez | deh-reh-gehz′ |
| | | Enweri | en′-weh-ree |
| i = ee | in bee | Iran | ee-rahn′ |
| | | Bushir | boo-sheer′ |
| | | Nizami | nee-zah′-mee |
| u = oo | in boot | Balfurush | bahl-foo-roosh′ |
| | | Kabul | kah-bool′ |
| | | Firdusi | feer-doo′-see |
| u = ŭ | in but | Tukhti | tŭch-h-tee′ |
| | | Sudup | sud-ŭp′ |
| | | | |
| ae = ah-eh | | Daeny | dah-eh-nee |
| ai = I | in pine | Kalaichi | kah-lI′-tchee |
| | | Nain | nIne |
| au = aw | in awe | Jowaur | jo-wawr′ |
| ay = I | in pine | Khayyam | ch-hI-yahm′ |
| ei = ā | in ale | Mei-omid | mā-o-meed′ |
| ey = ā | in ale | Neybundan | nā boon-dahn′ |
| ou = oo | in boot | Choubar | tchoo-bar′ |
| | | Souch-Bulak | sootch′-boo′-lahk |
| | | | |
| ch = tch | | Beloochistan | beh-loo-tchees-tahn′ |
| | | Cachar | kah-tchar′ |
| g = g | in get | Jagepur | jah-gheh-poor′ |
| | | Geuk Tepe | gā′-ook-teh′-peh |
| gh = g | in get | Ghizni | gheez-nee′ |
| | | Ghilan | ghee-lahn′ |
| j = j | | Jajarcote | jah jar-kōtē′ |
| | | Jajerm | jah jerm′ |
| kh = ch-h[1] | | Khorassan | ch-ho-rahs-sahn′ |
| | | Bakhtigan | bach-h-tee-gahn′ |

1. This sound is a harsh guttural. Grammars furnish no guide in respect to accent.

# INDIA.

| | | | |
|---|---|---|---|
| a = a | in ah | Allahabad | ah-lah-hah- bahd´ |
| | | Rajahmahal | rah-jah- mah- hal´ |
| e = e | in eh | Dera | deh´-rah |
| e = e | in bee | Pegu | pee-goo´ |
| i = I | in pin | Pinyaree | pin-yar´-ree |
| | | Bhindur | bin-door´ |
| u = oo[1] | in boot | Pegu | pee-goo´ |
| | | Punah | poo´-nah |
| u = ŭ | in bun | Punjab | pun´-jawb |
| | | Kupperwunje | kup-per-wŭnj´ |
| y = I | in pine | Gykwar | ghike´-war |
| | | Zyghur | zI-gŭr |
| y = ee | in bee | Bhowany | bō-wah´ nee |
| | | | |
| ae = ah-eh | | Rae | rah´-eh |
| ai = I | | Ismailbad | is-mIle-bahd |
| | | Laighpur | lIgh-poor´ |
| | | Jaitpur | jIte-poor´ |
| ao = ah-ŏ | | Khyrgaon | kIre gah-ŏn´ |
| au = aw | in awe | Ghauts | gawts |
| | | Awrungabad | aw-rung-gah-bahd´ |
| ay = I | | Chayenpoor | tchI-en-poor´ |
| | | Sandoway | sahn-do-wI´ |
| ea = eh-ah | | Beas | beh´-ahss |
| ei² = ā | in ale | Oojein | oo-jāne´ |
| | | Bassein | bahs sāne´ |
| ei = ee | in bee | Neilgherry | neel-gher´ ry |
| ey = ā | | Deypaulpoor | dā-pawl-poor´ |
| ey = I | | Jeypoor | jI poor´ |
| ie = ee | in bee | Dhamie | dah-mee´ |
| oa = o-ah | | Noanagur | no-ah nah-gŭr´ |
| | | Noapoora | no-ah-poo´-rah |
| ou = oo | in boot | Oudh | ood |
| ui = wee | | Guicowar | gwee-co-war´ |
| ui = ee | | Mergui | mer-ghee´ |
| ye = I | | Mhye | m'hI |
| | | Kassye-Gopang | kahs´-sI-go-pabng´ |

The spelling of Indian names here given is of course, in the main, English, yet is not without inconsistencies.  1. When it ends a syllable?  2. In names of Mahomedan origin?

## INDIA—Continued.

| | | | |
|---|---|---|---|
| bh = b | | Bhawlpoor | bawl-poor′ |
| | | Bhavani-Kudal | bah-vah′-nee-koo-dahl′ |
| ch¹ = tch | | Trichinopoly | tritch-in-op′-o-lee |
| | | Cheychun | tcha-tchoon′ |
| ch = sh | | Pondicherry | pon-dī-sher′-ree |
| g = g | in get | Gilghit | ghil-ghit′ |
| | | Gujerat | goo-zheh-raht′ |
| gui = gwi | | Guicowar | gwik-o-war′ |
| gui = ghee | | Mergui | mer-ghee′ |
| j = j | | Jaypoor | jī-poor′ |
| j = zh | | Gujerat | goo-zheh-raht′ |
| kh = ch-h² | | Khanhaila | ch-hahn-hī′-lah |
| | | Khair | ch-hīre |
| qu = kw | | Quilon | kwee-lon′ |
| | | Somnauth | som-nawt′ |
| th = t | | Thurr | turr |
| | | Tattha | taht′-tah |
| | | Warungul | wah-run-gul′ |
| w = w | | Wadwan | wahd-wahn′ |

x and z as in English

1. The sounds of *ch* and of *j* are believed to be more commonly those first given. 2. A guttural, an extremely rough *h*.

# CHINA.

| a = a | in ah | Pa | pah |
|---|---|---|---|
| | | Shara | shah′-rah′ |
| e = ā | in ale | Le | lā |
| e = ē | | Ke-lung | ke′-lung′ |
| e = ĕ | | Cheng-te | cheng′-tā′ |
| i = ee | | Li | lee |
| i = ĭ | | Chin-yuen | chĭn′-yoo-en′ |
| u = oo | | Fu | foo |
| u = ŭ | | Chung | chŭng |
| y = ee | | Tsun-y | tsŭn′-ee′ |
| | | Y-Chou | ee′-choo′ |
| | | | |
| ae = I | | Ting-hae | ting′-hI′ |
| | | Tong-lae | tong′-lI′ |
| ai = I | | Hoai | ho′-I′ |
| | | Ai-chow | I′-chow′ |
| ao = ah-o | | Macao | mah-cah′-o |
| | | Liao | lee′-ah′-o |
| au = ah-oo | | Matau | mah′-tah′-oo |
| | | Pitau | pee′-tah′-oo |
| ay = I | | Hiayntong | hee-Ine′-tong′ |
| | | Cayuen | cah′-yoo-en′ |
| ei = ā | | Hoei | ho′-ā′ |
| | | Pei-ho | pā′-ho′ |
| ia = ee-ah | | Ho-kian | ho′-kee-ahn′ |
| | | Che-kiang | cheh′-kee-ahng′ |
| ie = ee-eh | | Kien-Lung | kee-en′-lung′ |
| | | I-kien | ee′-kee-en′ |

## CHINA—Continued.

| | | |
|---|---|---|
| iu = ee-oo | Cha-kiu | chah'-kee-oo' |
| | Liu-chou | lee-oo'-choo' |
| oa = o-ah | Kai-hoa | kī'-ho-ah' |
| oe = o-ā | Wei-hoe | wā'-ho-ā' |
| ou = oo | Fou-Chou | foo'-choo' |
| | Hou-pe | hoo'-pā' |
| ua = oo-ah | Hua-Tsiang | hwah'-tsee-ang' |
| ue = oo-eh | Se-chuen | sā'-choo-en' |
| | Yuen-Tcheou | yoo-en'-choo' |
| ui = oo-ee | Lui-chow | loo-ee'-chow' |
| iao = ee-ah-o | Seng-miao-se | seng'-mee-ah'-o-sā' |
| iue = ee-oo-ā | Siuen-hwa | see oo-ān'-hwah' |
| uei = oo-ā | Kuei-Chou | koo-ā'-choo' |
| ouei = oo-ā | Sung-pan-ouei | sung-pan'-oo-ā' |
| eouoei = ā-oo-o-ā | Taolcheouoei | towl'-choo'-wā' |
| | | |
| ch = tch | Chi-ching | tchee'-tching |
| sz = ss | Szechuen | ssā'-choo-en' |

# JAPAN.

| | | | |
|---|---|---|---|
| a = a | in ah | Nagasaki | nah-gah-sah'-kee |
| | | Uraga | oo-rah'-gah |
| e = e | in eh | Yedegawa | yeh-deh-gah'-wah |
| | | Desima | deh'-see-mah |
| i = ee | in bee | Tokio | to-kee'-o |
| | | Itsi | eet'-see |
| u = oo | in boot | Fukurokudo | foo-koo-ro-koo'-do |
| | | Shikoku | shee-ko-koo' |
| y = ee | in bee | Gokynay | gō-kee-ni' |
| ae = I | in pine | Matsumae | maht-soo-mi' |
| ai = I | | Ashunkaido | ah-shoon-kI'-do |
| | | Poronai | po-ro-ni' |
| ay = I | | Saykaydo | sI-kI'-do |
| | | Nankaydo | nahn-kI'-do |
| eu = eh-oo | | Teuriogawa | teh-oo'-ree-e-gah'-wah |
| iu = ee-oo | | Kiushiu | kee-oo'-shee-oo' |
| | | Riukiu | ree-oo'-kee oo' |
| ou = oo | in boot | Inouye | ee-noo'-yeh |
| ch = tch | | Kawaguchi | kah-wah-goo'-tchee |
| | | Choshiu | tchō-shee-oo' |
| j = y | | Joritomo | yo-ree-to-mo |
| | | Kijomori | kee-yo-mo-ree |
| x = z | | Ximo | zee'-mo |

# NORTHERN ASIA.

| | | | |
|---|---|---|---|
| a = a | in ah | Anabara | ah-nah-bah-rah' |
| | | Abalak | ah bah-lahk' |
| e = e | in eh | Selenghinsk | seh-lehn gheensk' |
| | | Keta | keh'-tah |
| i = ee | in bee | Sir-i-Kol | seer-ee-kol' |
| | | Sibir | see-beer' |
| y = ee | in bee | Tsypa | tsee'-pah |
| | | Kolyma | ko-lee'-mah |
| u = oo | in boot | Surgut | soor-goot' |
| | | Ulungur | oo-loon-goor' |
| | | | |
| ai = ī | in pine | Baikal | bī'-kal |
| | | Tarbagatai | tar-bah-gah-tai' |
| ay = ī | in pine | Abatskaya | ah-bahts kī'-yah |
| | | Shayuk | shī-yook' |
| ei = ā | in ale | Alei | ah-lā' |
| | | Yeneseisk | yeh-nee seh'-eesk |
| ey = ā | in ale | Zeya | zā'-yah |
| ou = oo | in boot | Ouratepe | oo-rah-teh'-peh |
| ue = weh | | Kuenlun | kwen'-loon' |
| ui = oo-ee | | Viliui | vee-lee-oo'-ee |
| | | Jelagui | yeh-lah-goo'-ee |
| uj = oo-ee | | Aniuj | ah-nee-oo'-ee |
| uy = oo-ee | | Muya | moo-ee-ah |
| | | | |
| ch = tch | | Kamchatka | kahm-tchat'-kah |
| j = y-ee | | Jelagui | yeh-lah-goo'-ee |
| | | Wjatka | vee-aht'-kah |
| kh = ch-h | | Kiahkta | kee-ach-h'-tah |
| qu = koo | | Elaqui | eh-lah-koo'-ee |

1 A guttural, an extremely rough *k*.

# AFRICA.

| | | | |
|---|---|---|---|
| a = a | in ah | Amhara | ahm-hah'-rah |
| | | Namaqua | nah-mah'-quah |
| e = e | in eh | Medeah | meh-deh'-ah |
| | | Meroe | meh'-ro-eh |
| i = ee | in bee | Birbe | beer'-beh |
| | | Kebir | keh-beer' |
| u = oo | in book | Abu | ah'-boo |
| | | Siut | see-oot' |
| u = ŭ | in but | Mayumba | mah-yŭm'-bah |
| y = ee | in bee | Akhmym | ach-h-meem' |
| | | Rasulkhyle | rahs'-ool-ch-hee'-leh |
| y = ī | | Myos Hormos | mī'-os hor'-mos |
| ai = ī | | Cairo | kī'-ro |
| | | Ain | īne |
| au = ŏw | in cow | Ougila | ŏw-jee'-lah |
| | | El-Haura | el-how'-rah |
| ay = ī | | Fayoum | fī-oom' |
| | | Fanaye | fah-nī'-yeh |
| ea = eh-ah | | Enarea | eh-nah'-reh-ah |
| | | Narea | nah'-reh-ah |
| ei = ā | in ale | Kosseir | kos-sāre' |
| | | Sheik | shāke |
| ey = ā | in ale | Zeyla | zā'-lah |
| | | Seychelles | sā-shell' |
| ey = ī | | Graaf Reynet | grahf rī'-net |
| ie = ee-eh | | Ghindieh | gheen' dee-eh |
| | | Rahmanich | rah-mahn'-ee-eh |

## AFRICA—Continued.

| | | | |
|---|---|---|---|
| oe = ee | in bee | Moeris | mee'-ris |
| oë = o-eh | | Meroë | meh'-ro-eh |
| oe = oo | | Bloemhof | bloom'-hof |
| oe = o | | Arroe | ar-rō |
| oi = ee | in bee | Oibo | ee'-bo |
| ou = oo | | Aboukir | ah-boo-keer' |
| | | Ouad | oo-ahd' |
| ou = ŏw | in cow | Oudtshoorn | ŏwts'-horn |
| | | | |
| ch = tch | | Bechuana | bet-choo-ah'-nah |
| ch = sh | | Cherchell | sher-shell' |
| g = j | | Girgeh | jeer'-jeh |
| g = g | in get | Gizeh | ghee'-zeh |
| j = j | | Jebel | jeb'-el |
| j = zh | | Ajan | ah'-zhahn |
| lh = l'ye | | Ilheo | eel-yeh'-o |
| qu = k | | Querimba | keh reem'-bah |
| x = sh | | Magodoxa | mah-gah-do'-shah |
| z = ts | | Tacazze | tah-kaht'-seh |

The various powers of the same letters on this page may perhaps be made somewhat less perplexing by considering that they follow to a great extent the analogy of the several languages spoken by European colonists in Africa, and prevail especially, each in the region occupied by the corresponding race. The Dutch sound of *ae*, *oe*, *i*, *e*, *oo*, or of *ou*, namely *ŏw*, will occur chiefly among the Boers of South Africa; *ch* and *j* will be apt to have their English value in Egypt and at the Cape, their French and Portuguese elsewhere.

# SOUTH AMERICA.

| | | | |
|---|---|---|---|
| a = a | in ah | Alcantara | ahl-cahn-tah'-rah |
| | | Aymara | I-mah-rah' |
| c = c | in eh | Alegrette | ah-leh-gret'-teh |
| | | Cerea | seh-reh'-ah |
| i = ee | in bee | Chiriqui | chee-ree-kee' |
| | | Quito | kee'-to |
| u = oo | in boot | Cuzco | koos'-ko |
| | | Puno | poo'-no |
| y = ee | in bee | Yaracuy | ee-ah-rah-coo-ee' |
| | | Apihahy | ah-pee-ah'-ee |

| | | | |
|---|---|---|---|
| c¹ = c | in cell | Concepcion | con-sep-see-on' |
| ç = c | in cell | Conceicao | con-seh-ee-sah'-oh |
| ch = tch | | Chagres | tchah'-gres |
| | | Chiriqui | tchee-ree-kee' |
| g² = zh | | Sergipe | sair-zhee'-peh |
| g³ = h | | Cartagena | car-tah-heh'-nah |
| gu¹ = g | in get | Portuguesa | por-too-gheh'-sah |
| gu⁴ = gw | | Guajira | gwar-hee'-rah |
| h is silent | | Bahia | bah ee'-ah |
| | | Apihahy | ah-pee-ah'-ee |
| j⁵ = h | | Jujuy | hoo-hoo-ee' |
| j⁶ = zh | | Joazeiras | zho-ah-seh'-ee-rahss |
| lh = l'ye | | Velha | vehl'-yah |
| ll = l'ye | | Truxillo | troo-heel'-yo |
| nh = n'ye | | Maranhao | mah-rahn-yah'-o |
| | | Cunha | koon'-yah |
| qu = k | | Barquesimeta | bar-keh-see-meh'-tah |
| | | Arequipa | ah-reh kee'-pah |
| x⁶ = sh | | Abacaxis | ah-bah-cah-sheesh' |
| x⁵ = h | | Xabary | hah-bah-ree' |
| z = s | | Azul | ah-sool' |
| | | Zozoranga | so-so-rahn'-gah |

1. Before *e* and *ı*.  2. In Brazil before *e* and *i*.  3. Elsewhere before *e* and *i*.  4. Before *a* and *o*.  5. In Spanish colonies.  6. In Brazil. As will be inferred from the preceding notes, different values of the same letter or letters in South American names, are in general severally confined to countries settled by Spaniards and by Portuguese respectively.

## SOUTH AMERICA—Continued.

| | | | |
|---|---|---|---|
| ae = ah-eh | | Minas Geraes | mee'-nahss-zheh-rah'-es |
| | | Aimaraez | I-mah-rah'-es |
| ai = I | | Valparaiso | vahl-pah-rI'-so |
| ao = ah-o | | Sao Paulo | sah-o-pow'-lo |
| | | Callao | cahl-lah'-o |
| au = ŏw | in cow | Piauhi | pee-ow'-ee |
| | | Maule | mow'-leh |
| ay = I | | Buenos Ayres | boo-eh'-noce I'-res |
| | | Uruguay | oo-roo-gwI' |
| ea = eh-ah | | Aldea | ahl-deh'-ah |
| | | Breas | breh'-ahss |
| ei = eh-ee | | Almeida | ahl-meh' ee-dah |
| | | Gualateiri | gwar-lah-teh'-ee-ree |
| eu = eh-oo | | Euzebio | eh-oo-seh'-bee o |
| | | Neuguen | neh-oo-ghen' |
| ey = eh-ee | | Guarmey | gwar-meh'-ee |
| | | Yapeyu | ee-ah-peh'-ee-oo |
| ie = ee-eh | | Diego | dee-eh'-go |
| | | Cienega | see-eh-neh'-gah |
| oa = o-ah | | Agoaquente | ah-go-ah-ken'-teh |
| oe = o-eh | | Chiloe | chee-lo-eh' |
| | | Oeiras | o eh-ee'-rahss |
| oe¹ = oo | | Welgemoed | vel-geh-mood |
| ou = oo | | Outeiro | oo teh'-ee-ro |
| | | Ouya | oo'-yah |
| ua = oo-ah | | Huawra | oo-ăw'-rah |
| | | Guaduas | goo ah'-doo-ahss |
| ue = oo-eh | | Buen Ayr | boo-ehn'-Ire' |
| | | Llanquihue | lahn-kee' oo-eh |
| ui = oo-ee | | Uirubu | oo-ee-roo'-boo |
| | | Buines | boo-ee'-nes |
| uy = oo-ee | | Yaracuy | ee-ah rah koo-ee' |
| | | Apatuya | ah-pah-too-ee'-ah |

1. In Dutch Guiana.

# MEXICO AND CENTRAL AMERICA.

| | | | |
|---|---|---|---|
| a = a | in ah | Tlahs-cah-lah | tlahs-cah'-lah |
| | | Canada | cahn-yah'-dah |
| e = e | in eh | Tepeje | teh-peh'-heh |
| | | Velen | veh-lehn' |
| i = ee | in bee | Chiquihuita | tchee-kee wee'-tah |
| | | Sinoquipa | see-no-kee'-pah |
| u = oo | in boot | Churubusco | tchoo-roo boos'-ko |
| | | Catuno | cah-toon'-yo |
| y = ee | in bee | Cuynaco | coo-ee-oo-ah' co |
| ai = I | | Fraile | frI'-leh |
| | | El Maiz | el mIze |
| au = ŏw | in cow | Tamaulipas | tah-mow-lee'-pahs |
| | | San Augustine | sahn ŏw-goos teen |
| ay = I | | Guaymas | gwI'-mahss |
| ea = eh-ah | | Tepeaca | teh-peh-ah'-cah |
| ei = ā | | Teipan | tā-pahn' |
| eo = ah-o | | Teotihuacan | teh o-tee-hwah-cahn |
| eu = eh-oo | | Teul | teh ool' |
| ey = ā | | Tepeyahualco | teh-pā-ah-wahl'-c |
| ie = ee-eh | | San Diego | sahn-dee-eh'-go |
| oa = o-ah | | Oajaca | o-ah-hah'-cah |
| ou = oo | in boot | Guadaloupe | gwah dah-loo'-pe |
| ua = wah | | Tehuantepec | teh-wahn-teh-pee |
| ue = weh | | Huehuetoca | weh-weh-to'-cah |
| ui = wee | | Coahuila | co-ah-wee'-lah |

## MEXICO AND CENTRAL AMERICA—Continued.

| | | |
|---|---|---|
| c   as in English | Cerrocahui | ser-ro-cah-wee′ |
| cc = k-s | Iztaccihuatl | ecz-tak-see-wahtl′ |
| ch = tch | Michoacan | mee-cho ah-cahn′ |
| g = h | Gigedo | hee-heh′-do |
| h  is silent | Hiaqui | ee-ah′-kee |
| j = h | Jalapa | hah-lah′-pah |
| ll = l′ye | Fresnilla | fres neel′-yah |
| n = ni        in minion | Pinos | peen′-yoce |
| qu = k | Queretaro | keh-reh-tah′-ro |
| x = h | Xochitepec | ho-tchee-teh pec′ |
| x = x | Ixcaquiktla | eex-cah-keex′-tlah |
| z = s[1] | Zacatecas | sah-cah-teh′-cahss |

1, When initial?

# UNITED STATES.

| | |
|---|---|
| Abiquiu | ah-bee-kee-oo' |
| Abilene | 'ah'-bĭ-lene |
| Aboite | ah-boit |
| Abrego | ahb'-re-go |
| Absecom | ab-se'-kom |
| Acequia | ah-sā'-kee-ah |
| Achor | ā'-kor |
| Acquia | ah-kee'-ah |
| Acushnet | ah-kwish'-net |
| Adobe | ah-do'-beh |
| Ai | I |
| Alachua | ah-latch'-u-ah |
| Alafia | ah-lah-fee'-ah |
| Alameda | ah-lah-mā'-dah |
| Alamo | ah'-lah-mo |
| Alapaha | ah-lap'-a-haw |
| Alaqua | ah-la'-quaw |
| Albuquerque | ahl-boo-kaĭr'-keh |
| Alekmagek | ahl-ek-nah-gek' |
| Alfonte | ahl-font' |
| Aline | ah-leen' |
| Allamakee | ah-lah-mah-kee' |
| Alleguash | ahl'-leh-gash |
| Almoral | ahl-mo-ral' |
| Alquina | ahl-kee'-nah |
| Amatiguak | ah-mah-tee-guak' |
| Amissville | ā' miss-vil |
| Amite | am-eet' |
| Apache | ah-pah'-tcheh |
| Apotacon | ah-po'-tah-kon |
| Armuchee | ar-muk'-ee |
| Aswabanon | a-swob'-a-non |
| Attoyac | at-to-yak' |
| Audrain | aw'-drāne |
| Au Gres | ō-grāze' |
| Avayelles | ah-vi'-el |
| Ballyclough | bal-ly-kloh' |
| Bangall | ban-gall' |
| Bernice | ber-'nĭce |
| Bevier | be-veer' |

## UNITED STATES—Continued.

| | |
|---|---|
| Bexar | ba-har' |
| Bijou | bee-zhoo' |
| Bodcau | bod'-kŏw |
| Bodega | bo-dā'-ga |
| Boerchenville | ber'-chen-vil |
| Boerne | berne |
| Bonhomme | bon-hom' |
| Boscawen | bos'-kwoin |
| Botetourt | bo'-teh-tort |
| Boughton | bŏw'-ton |
| Broughton | brō'-ton |
| Bryn Mawr | brin-mar' |
| Butte | bûte |
| Calcasieu | cal' ca-shu |
| Caneadea | ca-ne-ă'-de-a |
| Caughdenoy | kok-e-nay' |
| Chagreen | sha-green |
| Chamois | sham'-me |
| Chautauque | sha-taw'-que |
| Chebanse | she-banss' |
| Chebeagae | she-beeg' |
| Chemung | she-mung' |
| Chetopa | she-to'-pa |
| Chiques | chik'-kiz |
| Chino | shee'-no |
| Chireno | shee-ra'-no |
| Chisago | chee-saw'-go |
| Chocolay | cho-co'-lay |
| Chocorua | cho-co-ru'-a |
| Choestoe | cho'-sto |
| Chotean | cho'-teen |
| Chowan | chō-wan' |
| Cimarron | see-mar-ron' |
| Claverack | claw'-ve-rak |
| Cloutierville | kloo'-ti-er-vil |
| Cocolamus | ko-ko-law'-mus |
| Coeymans | kwee'-mans |
| Colita | ko-lee'-ta |
| Comanche | ko-man'-sheh |
| Conecah | ko-nee'-kah |
| Conejos | ko-nă'-hoce |
| Coos | ko-os' |
| Cowan | kow'-an |
| Cowanesque | kow-an-es'-que |
| Cowekee | kow-e-kee' |
| Coweta | kow-e'-ta |

## UNITED STATES—Continued.

| | |
|---|---|
| Cuyahoga | kI-a-hō'-ga |
| Decorah | de-ko'-rah |
| Devereux | dev-er-o' |
| Duelm | dwelm |
| Dunleith | dun-leeth |
| Easley | ees'-ly |
| Farquhar | far'-kar |
| Gila | hee'-la |
| Graneros | grah-nä'-roce |
| Gratiot | grah'-she-ŏt |
| Guionsville | ghI'-ons-vil |
| Haidee | hI'-dee |
| Hauppauge | hop'-pog |
| Hochheim | hok'-hime |
| Houcktown | howk'-town |
| Huerfano | hwer-fah'-no |
| Inistiog | In-is-tI-ōg' |
| Ischua | Ish'-u-a |
| Kinnickkinnick' | |
| Kittanning | kIt-tan'-ning |
| Kouts | kowts |
| Leigh | lee |
| Lenape | len-ahp' |
| Lenawee | len'-a-wee |
| Leuden | li'-den |
| Lonoke | lo-noke' |
| Loughborough | luf'-bö-rö |
| Mac Cune | mac-kun' |
| Mac Cleod | mac-loud' |
| Manicouagan | man-ni-kwah'-gahn |
| Manidowish | man-ni-do-wIsh' |
| Manitowoc | man-ni-to-woc' |
| Manteo | man-te'-o |
| Manteno | man-te'-no |
| Maringouin | mah-ranh-gwanh' |
| Massapeag | mas-sa-peg' |
| Mesquite | mes'-keet |
| Metomen | meh-to'-men |
| Metuchen | me-tutch'-en |
| Moe | mo |
| Mokelumne | mo-kel'-um-ne |
| Monocacy | mo-nok'-a-cy |
| Monteith | mon'-teeth |
| Mt. Guyot | ghee-o |
| Moweaqua | mow'-ä-qua |
| Muscogee | mus-co-ghee' |

## UNITED STATES—Continued.

| | |
|---|---|
| Musconetcong | mus-co-net'-coug |
| Missequogue | mis-se-quog' |
| Noxapata | nox-ah-pah'-tah |
| Nueces | nwā'-ces |
| Ochlochnee | ok-lok'-nee |
| Oconomowok | o-ko-nom'-o-wok |
| Okeechobee | o-kee-cho'-bee |
| Olean | o-le-an' |
| Olequa | o-le'-qua |
| Onekama | o-nek'-a-ma |
| Oquirrh | o-quer |
| Ouleout | owl'-e-owt |
| Pajaro | pah-hah'-ro |
| Papevert | pahp-vair' |
| Paotone | pah'-o-tone |
| Pequea | pek-wā' |
| Perquimans | per-quim'-ans |
| Pioche | pee-o'-cheh |
| Plaquemine | plak'-meen' |
| Pohono | po-ho'-no |
| Presque Isle | presk'-eel' |
| Punta Arenas | poon'-tah-ah-rā'-nahs |
| Queneno | keh-nee'-no |
| Quewhiffle | kwee-whifi' |
| Quinaiutt | kwee'-nI-ut |
| Ramapo | rah-mah-po' |
| Rickreal | rĭck-re-all' |
| Rio Grande | ree'-o-grahn'-deh |
| Rio Virgen | ree'-o veer-hūne' |
| Rosbach | ross'-bach-h |
| Rothsvillle | rōts'-vil |
| Rousseau | roo-sō' |
| Rowan | ro-wan' |
| Rutherford | rŭth'-er-ford |
| Saco | saw-ko |
| Saguache | sah'-watch' |
| Salina | sah-lee'-nah |
| Salkchatchie | sawl-ke-hatch-ee |
| San Augustine | sahn-ŏw-goos-teen' |
| San Diego | sahn-dee-ā'-go |
| Sangre de Christo | sahn'-grā-deh-krees'-to |
| San Joaquin | sahn-wah-keen' |
| San Jose | sahn ho-sa' |
| San Juan | sahn hoo-ahn' |
| Saint Augustin | st-aw-gus'-tin |
| Saucelito | saw-sel-ee'-to |

## UNITED STATES—Continued.

| | |
|---|---|
| Schley | shlI |
| Schoodie | skoo'-die |
| Schroeppel | skroo'-pel |
| Schroon | skroon |
| Schuyler | skI'-ler |
| Schuylkill | skool'-kil |
| Scituate | sit'-u-ate |
| Searcy | ser'-see |
| Seattle | see-at'-tle |
| Sebewa | seb'-e-wah |
| Sequin | se-gwin' |
| Sequin | sa-gheen' |
| Sehome | se-home |
| Seiad | sā'-ahd |
| Sevier | se-veer' |
| Sewanee | seh-wah'-nee |
| Seymour | seem'-er |
| Shawangunk | shong'-gum |
| Shawano | shah-wah'-no |
| Shayuen | shā-yu-en' |
| Shiawassee | shI-a-was'-see |
| Shoshone | sho-sho'-nee |
| Shubuta | shu-bu'-tah |
| Shumagine | shu-mah-gheen' |
| Sineaths | sI-neaths' |
| Singac | sIn'-jak |
| Sioux | soo |
| Siskiyu | sis-kee-yoo |
| Skohomish | sko-ho'-mish |
| Snachwine | snahk-wine |
| Soledad | so-le-dad' |
| Solgohachea | sol-go-hatch'-ee |
| Somonauk | so-mo-nawk' |
| Soquel | so-kel' |
| Spokane | spo'-kahn |
| Spuyten Duyvel | spI'-ten-dI'-vel |
| Stadakana | stah-dah-kah'-nah |
| Stanislaus | stahn-is-lŏw' |
| Stecoah | stek'-wah |
| Struthers | strŭth'-ers |
| Suamiko | swom'-i-ko |
| Suisun | soo-ee-soon' |
| Suwanee | swaw'-nee |
| Talmadge | tel'-mij |
| Tanaga | tah-nah'-gah |
| Tangipahoa | tahn-gI-pah-ho' |

## UNITED STATES—Continued.

| | |
|---|---|
| Taughgannock | taw-gan'-nok |
| Tchama | te-hah'-ma |
| Teheran | te-hē'-ran |
| Tekama | te-kah'-ma |
| Terre Coupé | tair'-koo-pā' |
| Thiry Daens | tir-ee-dāmz |
| Tidioute | tid-i-oot' |
| Tioughnioga | tee-o-nee-aw'-gah |
| Tomaha | to-mah-haw' |
| Tooele | too-el'-e |
| Tortuga | tor-too'-gah |
| Towaliga | to-wol'-i-gah |
| Treichler | trik'-ler |
| Tualatin | twol'-a-tin |
| Tunkhannock | tunk-haw'-nok |
| Twolumne | twol'-um-ne |
| Tygh | ti |
| Tymochtee | ti-mok'-tee |
| Uhlersville | ū-lers-vil |
| Uintah | ū-in'-tah |
| Unaka | ū'-nah-kah |
| Unitia | ū-nish'-e-ah |
| Upatoi | ū'-pa-toi |
| Urland | oor'-land |
| Volatie | vol'-a-she |
| Vallejo | val-yā'-ho |
| Vinita | vee'-nee-tah |
| Wahalak | waw-hah'-lak |
| Wahkiakum | wah-kee-ah'-kum |
| Wakatomica | wah-kah-tom'-i-kah |
| Waneka | wah-ne'-kah |
| Wapakoneta | wah-pah-ko-net'-ah |
| Wapsinonoc | wahp-sin'-o-nok |
| Wapsipinikon | wahp-si-pin'-i-kon |
| Waraju | wah-rah-ju' |
| Wapwallopen | wahp-wal-lo'-pen |
| Waseca | wah-se'-kah |
| Wasepi | was'-e-pee |
| Wasioja | was-ee-o'-jah |
| Wataga | wah-tah'-gah |
| Watauga | wah-taw'-gah |
| Watchemoket | wat-che-mo'-ket |
| Wathena | wath-e'-na |
| Watonwan | wah'-ten-wan |
| Watopa | wah-to'-pah |
| Waubesa | waw-be'-sa |

## UNITED STATES—Continued.

| | |
|---|---|
| Waucoma | wau-ko'-mah |
| Waucousta | waw-koos'-tah |
| Wau-hillau | waw-hil-law' |
| Waukecheen | waw'-ke-sheen |
| Waukesha | waw'-ke-sha |
| Wau-paka | waw-pah'-kah |
| Waupecong | waw'-pe-kong |
| Wauponsee | waw-pon-see' |
| Waupoun | waw-pŭn' |
| Wauregan | waw-re'-gahn |
| Wauscou | waw'-se-oo |
| Wausemon | waw'-se-mon |
| Waushara | waw-shah'-ra |
| Wautoma | waw-to'-ma |
| Wawaka | wah-wah'-ka |
| Wayzata | wI-zah'-ta |
| Wea | we'-a |
| Weare | wãre |
| Wedowee | we-dŏw'-ee |
| Weegee | wee-gee' |
| Weir | weer |
| Wekiva | we-kI'-va |
| Weyanoke | wI'-a-noke |
| Weyauwega | wI'-aw-we'-ga |
| Weybridge | wã'-bridge |
| Weymouth | wã'-mŭth |
| Wiandotte | wI'-an-dot' |
| Wickacanee | wik-kah-kah-nee' |
| Wicomico | wee-kom'-ee-ko |
| Willamette | wil-lahm'-et |
| Winamak | win'-a-mahk |
| Wingett | win'-jet |
| Winibigoshish | win-I-bI-go'-shish |
| Winipiseogee | win-nI-pI-saw'-kee |
| Winterroud | win'-ter-rōde |
| Wyoming | wI-ō'-ming |
| Yakima | yak'-ee-ma |
| Yavapai | yahv'-a-pI |
| Yosemite | yo-sem'-ee-te |
| Youghiogheny | yo-ho-gã'-ny |

# BRITISH AMERICA.

| | |
|---|---|
| Abatagoush | ah-bah-tah-goosh′ |
| Abatagomaw | ah-bah-tah-go′-maw |
| Ashwanipi | ash-wah-nip′-pee |
| Asimagomy | as-i-mah-go′-me |
| Ayton | I′-ton |
| Betsiamites | bet-see-ah-meet′ |
| Bersimis | bair-see-mee′ |
| Bobcaygeon | bob-ka′-jun |
| Chignegti | sheeg-neg′-te |
| Chertsey | ches-sy |
| Chebogomon | she-bo′-go-moo |
| Chicoutimi | shee-koo-tee-me′ |
| Clachan | clah′-ch-hahn |
| Clachnaharry | clach′-h-na-har′-ry |
| Coaticook | co-ah′-tee-cook |
| Contrecoeur | kontr′-kör |
| Cawatchan | cow-e-chan′ |
| Crapaud | crah-pō′ |
| Daillebut | dā′-ye′-boo′ |
| Dulwich | dul′-lich |
| Gananoque | gan-an-ōk′ |
| Gaultois | gole′-twoh′ |
| Golthaab | got-hahb |
| Hochelaga | ho-ke-lah′-ga |
| Isle au Carrot | eel′-o-car-rō′ |
| Isle au Chat | eel′-o-shah |
| Isle au Haut | eel′-o-hō′ |
| Isle au Heron | eel′-o-hā-ronh′ |
| Isle au Raisin | eel′-ō-rā-zänh′ |
| Isle au Sepulchre | eel-o-sā-pŭlkr′ |
| Isle au Chiens | eel-o-shee-änh′ |
| Isle aux Coudres | eel-o-koodr′ |
| Isle aux Grues | eel-o-grŭ′ |
| Isle aux Noix | eel-o-nwah′ |
| Isle aux Reaux | eel-o-rō′ |
| Isle aux Tetes | eel-o-tait′ |
| Isle Bizard | eel-bee-zarr′ |
| Isle Dupas | eel-du-pah′ |
| Isle la Peche | eel-lah-paish′ |
| Kenogami | ke-nog′-a-mee |
| Killean | kil-le-ahn′ |

## BRITISH AMERICA—Continued.

| | |
|---|---|
| Leith | leeth |
| Loughborough | lŏ'-bö-rö |
| MacLeod | mac-loud' |
| Manitowic | man-i-tŏw'-ik |
| Maurice | mŏ'-reess' |
| Metabetchouan | met-a-bet-choo-ahn |
| Metaghan | met-a-gh-han' |
| Methye | meh-thī' |
| Michel | mee'-shel' |
| Nassagaweya | nahs-sah-gah-wā'-yah |
| Nerepis | neh'-reh-pee |
| Penetanguechine | pen-eh-tahn'-geh-sheen |
| Pie de Deguire | pee'-deh-deh-gheer' |
| Quirpon | keer'-ponh' |
| Restigouche | restigoosh |
| Rochs | rösh |
| Saguenay | sag'-e-nā |
| Saint Aimé | sănh'-tā-mā' |
| Saint Alexandre | sănh' ahl-eks-onh-dr |
| Saint Andre | sănh' onh'-drā' |
| Saint Anices | sănh' ah'-neess |
| Saint Anselm | sănh' onh'-selm' |
| Saint Antoine | sănh' onh'-twawn' |
| Saint Antoine de Tilly | sănh' onh'-twawn'-deh'-tee'-yee' |
| Saint Antonin | sănh' onh-to-nănh |
| Saint Arsene | sănh' ar-sāne' |
| Saint Athanase | sănh' ah-tah-nahs' |
| Saint Aubert | sănh' ō-bair |
| Saint Augustin | sănh' ō-gŭs-tănh' |
| Saint Basil | sănh' bah-zeel' |
| Saint Bonaventure | sănh' bo-na-vonh-ture' |
| Saint Croix | sănh' krwaw' |
| Saint Cyrille | sănh' see-reel' |
| Saint Cyrille de la Pocatiere | sănh' see-reel'-deh-lah-po-cah-tee-air' |
| Saint Baume | sănh' bōme |
| Saint Brigide | sănh' bree-zheed' |
| Saint Foy | sănh' fwaw |
| Saint Gervais | sănh' zhair-vā' |
| Saint Jean d'Angely | sănh' zhanh-donh-zhe-lee' |
| Saskatchewan | sas-katch'-e-wan |
| Semisopochnoi | seh-mee-so-poch-h-noi |
| Stikine | stee-keen' |
| Temiscamingue | teh-mis-cah-ming' |
| Tsouuouthouan | tsoo-non-thoo-ahn' |
| Washademook | wash-a-de-mōke' |
| Whycoco'mah | |

# ENGLAND, SCOTLAND, AND IRELAND.

| | |
|---|---|
| Abbeyfeale | ab-be-fāle′ |
| Abbeyleix | ab-be-lāce′ |
| Abergavenny | ah′-ber-ghen-ny |
| Abergele | ah′-ber-ghee′-leh |
| Abersychan | ah′-ber-sŭck′-an |
| Accom | yac′-cam |
| Achill | ach-h′-ill |
| Adovalton | ath′-er-ton |
| Achonry | ach-h′-on-ry |
| Aghrim | awgh-h-reem′ |
| Ailsa | āle′-sa |
| Air | air |
| Alcester | aws′-ter |
| Alde | ald |
| Aldenley Edge | aud′-ly-edge′ |
| Alderwasley | al′-lers-ly |
| Almond | ah′-mond |
| Almondbury | am′-bry |
| Alne | horn |
| Alnwick | an′-nik |
| Alsager | au-ger |
| Althorp | all′-thorp |
| Altrincham | thrutchm |
| | antrinjam |
| | altringam |
| | antsjam |
| Altringham | all′-tring-ham |
| Alvanley | awvanly |
| Alwoodley Gate | anley gate |
| Amotherby | em′-mer-by |
| Aoon | orn |
| Argyle | ar′-ghīle |
| Arlecdon | arl′-ton |
| Armagh | ar-mahgh′ |
| Arundel | arndle |
| Ashburnham | esh′-brum |
| Ashton-under-Lyne | aeshin |
| Askeaton | as-kā′-ton |

## ENGLAND, SCOTLAND, AND
## IRELAND—Continued.

| | |
|---|---|
| Athboy' | |
| Athelbampstone | ath'-el-tun |
| Athy | ah-thi' |
| Auchinleck | af-flek |
| Auchtermuchty | och-h-ter-much-h-ty |
| Aughton | i-tun |
| Auldearn | owl-dairn |
| Avrton Gifford | autun jiffud |
| Aylesbure | alez-ber-ry |
| Ayr | air |
| Ayscough | as-key |
| Ayton | yatton |
| Babingley | beverley |
| Balguy | borgy |
| Balmo'ral | |
| Balquhitter | bal-kit-ter |
| Banff | banf |
| Barfrestone | barsn |
| Barugh | bark |
| Beaconsfield | bek-onz-feld |
| Beauchamp | beechm |
| Beauchief | beechif |
| Beaulieu | bewly |
| Beekbrook | beg-brook |
| Bedel | biddel |
| Beeston | beesn |
| Beith | beeth |
| Bellingham | bellinjam |
| Belvoir | beevor |
| Berkeley | barkly |
| Berwick | berrik |
| Bicester | bister |
| Bethune | beatun |
| Bligh | bli |
| Blythe | bli |
| Bollington | bollitn |
| Booth Town | boors-town |
| Bovey Tracey | buvvy |
| Brampton Brian | brawn |
| Brassington | brassn |
| Breaston | breesn |
| Brighthelmston | bryton |
| Bridlington | burlington |
| Brislington | busten |

## ENGLAND, SCOTLAND, AND
### IRELAND—Continued.

| | |
|---|---|
| Brompton | brumpton |
| Brough | bruf |
| Brougham | broom |
| Broughton | brukton |
| Broune | broon |
| Buccleuch | buk-klu |
| Bucklow Hill | bukly hil |
| Bullingham | bullinjm |
| Burgh | bruf |
| Bylaugh | bee-lo |
| Cadogan | caddugun |
| Calne | cone |
| Calva | cova |
| Carlisle | carell |
| Carshalton | casehalton |
| Carsington | carsn |
| Caverham | ca-num |
| Cawston | carsun |
| Chaddesden | chadsn |
| Chatham | chattum |
| Charteris | charters |
| Cheadle Hulme | cheddle eume |
| Chelmsford | chemzford |
| Chertsey | chessy |
| Chidcock | chid-dik |
| Chiswick | chiz-zik |
| Cholmondelsy | chumly |
| Cholmondeston | chumston |
| Cirencester | ciziter |
| | serenster |
| Claverly | clarely |
| Cleckheaton | klek-e-ton |
| Cley | klee |
| Clough | cluff |
| Clowyd | cloo-id |
| Clytha | kluth-a |
| Cockburn | co'-burn |
| Cogshall | cockshal |
| Coke | cook |
| Colclough | cokeley |
| Coln | kōn |
| Colquhoun | co-hoon' |
| Colteshall | colesl |
| Colwick | collik |

## ENGLAND, SCOTLAND, AND
## IRELAND—Continued.

| | |
|---|---|
| Colwick | college |
| Colzean | cŏlzäne' |
| Compton | cumton |
| Congleston | congerton |
| Cosham | coo-ham |
| Costessy | cossy |
| Coutts | coots |
| Cowper | cooper |
| Coxwold | cookwood |
| Craigneish | crāig'-nish |
| Craignethan | craig-neth'-an |
| Creagh | crā-gh-h |
| Crediton | kirtum |
| Cre Fydd | griffith |
| Cromford | crumford |
| Cumnock | cum-lok |
| Dalburg | dolberry |
| Dalziel | deell |
| Dartmoor | dartymor |
| Davenham | dane-um |
| Daventry | dauntry |
| | danetry |
| Derby | darby |
| Derrygheighan | derry-hā'-han |
| Derwent | darrant |
| Donnington | dunnington |
| Dove | dōve |
| Duls Coppice | doo-cups |
| Durham | dorm |
| Eardswick | yarsick |
| Easkey | āse-ky |
| Easley | ees-ly |
| Eig | eeg |
| Eisdale | ees-dale |
| Etruria | trury |
| Eyam | eem |
| Fangfoss | fankess |
| Featherstonehaugh | featherstun |
| Foljambe | fulljm |
| Fox le Henning | foxnailin |
| Frodsham | fradsum |
| Frome | frume |
| Gifford | jiffud |
| Glamis | glamz |

## ENGLAND, SCOTLAND, AND
## IRELAND—Continued.

| | |
|---|---|
| Glaston | glasn |
| Glencoin | lenkerrin |
| Glyndyfwydwy | glindowdwy |
| Gough | goff |
| Gould | gold |
| Grappenhall | gropnall |
| Guerin | geering |
| Guiseley | ghizly |
| Hague | haig |
| Haigh | haig |
| Hallahon } Hollon } | horn |
| Halton | hawton |
| Happisburgh | hazeboro |
| Hardwick | hardik |
| Harewood | harwood |
| Hautbois | hobbies |
| Haworden | hardn |
| | hordn |
| Hawes | hose |
| Hawick | hoick |
| Heathcote | heth-cut |
| Heigham | hayum |
| Herries | harris |
| Hertford | harford |
| Hobart | hubbert |
| Holborn | hoborn |
| Holmes Chapel | hoomz chapel |
| Horningsea | hornsy |
| Hotham | huthm |
| Hough | huff |
| Hughenden | hitchendon |
| Hull Senna | ho sena |
| Hunmanby | hunnenby |
| Hunstanton | hunston |
| Idridgehay | ithersy |
| Ilfracombe | il'-fracoom |
| Ilkeston | ilson |
| Ingonish | in-go-nish' |
| Innishgeil | Innishgheel' |
| Innishkea | innishkā' |
| Innishtogue | innishtōg' |
| Jedburgh | jethart |
| Kedleston | kelsn |

## ENGLAND, SCOTLAND, AND
### IRELAND—Continued.

| | |
|---|---|
| Keighley | keethly |
| Keir | keer |
| Kelsall | kelsa |
| Kelswick | kelsik |
| Kenilworth | killingworth |
| Kerr | karr |
| Kersley | karsly |
| Kidderminster | kiddy |
| Killaloe | killaloo' |
| Killyleigh | killylā' |
| Kilsyth | kilsīthe' |
| Kincard'ne | kincar'din |
| Kinross | kin-ross' |
| Kircudbright | kirkoobry |
| Kirkleavington | kilton |
| Kirriemuir | kirrimure |
| Knollys | noles |
| Laslett | lacy |
| Launceston | lausu |
| Leamington | lemington |
| Legard | ledjud |
| Leicester | lester |
| Leigh | lee |
| Leitrim | leetrim |
| Leith | leeth |
| Leominster | lemster |
| Levison-Gower | lewson-gore |
| Linlithgow | linlith'-gō |
| Linthwaite | linfit |
| Litchurch | leechurch |
| Loch Achray | loch-h-ach-hrā' |
| Loch na Sealg | loch-h-nah sailg' |
| Lostwithiel | lostwith'-el |
| Lougborough | luf'-bö-rö |
| Lough Neach | loch-h-nā' |
| Loughrea | loch-h-rā' |
| Ludgvan | lid'-gen |
| Macclesfield | maxfield |
| | maxfilt |
| | maxlt |
| Mackay | mackie |
| | ma-kā' |
| Macleod | maccloud |
| Mahon | mahoun |

## ENGLAND, SCOTLAND, AND
## IRELAND—Continued.

| | |
|---|---|
| Mainwaring | mannering |
| Malling | marling |
| Malpas | mawpus |
| Maucester | mansetter |
| Marjoribanks | marchbanks |
| Marylebone | marrybone |
| Marlboro | morlbro |
| Marston | marsn |
| Marylebone | marrowbone |
| Meigle | meegl |
| Menzies | mingis |
| Meredydd | merdith |
| Methven | meffin |
| Moncidie | mon-e-dee |
| Mohoun | moon |
| Monteith | monteeth' |
| Nuneaton | yeaton |
| Oakhampton | ockington |
| Odiham | odium |
| Oldham | ŏwdam |
| Ollerton | ŏwlerton |
| Oversley | oozly |
| Ouchter | ŏchter |
| Oughtrington | ootrington |
| Palk | park |
| Pampisford | pancher ' |
| Penicuik | pen-e-kük |
| Penrith | perith |
| | peerith |
| Peover | peever |
| Pevensey | pinsey |
| Pleasley | plezly |
| Plemondstall | plemstall |
| Pole | pool |
| Ponsonby | punsnby |
| Pontefract | pomfret |
| Powell | po-ell |
| Powlett | porlet |
| Puleston | pilston |
| Quarn | quorn |
| Quarndon | quorn |
| Rachlin | rachlin |
| Raleigh | raw-ly |
| Ramelton | ramelton |

## ENGLAND, SCOTLAND, AND
### IRELAND—Continued.

| | |
|---|---|
| Rasay | rah'-sā |
| Rathangan | rathan'-gan |
| Rathkeale | rathkail' |
| Ravenstone | rarnston |
| Rievaulx | rivis |
| Rocester | roaster |
| Rolleston | roleston |
| Roscrea | roscrā' |
| Rosewain | rosnan |
| Rostherne | rostern |
| Rothes | rŏth'-es |
| Rothesay | roth'-e-sā |
| Rouse | rūse |
| Routen | rooten |
| Rowrah | roora |
| Rowsley | rosely |
| Rutherglen | ruth |
| Ruthven | riven |
| Saint Clair | sinclair |
| Saint Ives | sent eves |
| Saint John | senjin |
| Saint Leger | sellinger |
| Saint Maur | seemer |
| Saint Neots | senneets' |
| Salhouse | sallus |
| Salisbury | sawlzberry |
| Salle | sorl |
| Sandiacre | senjyker |
| Sandwith | sanith |
| Sawbridgeworth | sawcer |
| Scafell | scaufel |
| Sciennes | sheens |
| Scone | scoon |
| Scropton | scrapn |
| Scuir of Eigg | skūre ov eeg |
| Seil | seel |
| Shepton | shepon |
| Shrewsbury | shrose-bry |
| Shurlach | surlash |
| Sidmouth | sidmuth |
| Skaldersken | skoderska |
| Skeyton | skytn |
| Slaithwaite | slawet |
| Sligo | slīgo |

ENGLAND, SCOTLAND, AND
IRELAND—Continued.

| | |
|---|---|
| Slough | slou |
| Sneyd | sneed |
| Southwark | sutherk |
| Southwell | suthell |
| Sowerby | soresby |
| Spondon | spoondon |
| Sproston | spros'n |
| Stockport | stoppart |
| Stonehewer | stannier |
| Stourbridge | stoor |
| Stourport | stoorport |
| Strachan | strorn |
| Strathaven | strathown |
| Swarkaston | swarsn |
| Teathes | teaz |
| Teignmouth | tinmuth |
| Thurleston | thurlsn |
| Thwaite | twait |
| Thynne | tin |
| Timoleague | timolaig |
| Tinehely | tin-hee-ly |
| Tintagel | tin-tadgel |
| Torquay | tor-kee |
| Towcester | toster |
| Trevelyan | trevethlan |
| Turnditch | tunditch |
| Twickenham | twittenham |
| Uist | wist |
| Uttoxeter | tuxeter |
| | uxeter |
| Uyea | oo-ya |
| Vaulx | vorx |
| Walsingham | walsicum |
| Warwick | warrik |
| Wavertree | wartree |
| Weald | weeld |
| Wear | weer |
| Weaverham | wearum |
| Wednesburg | wenzbry |
| Wemys | weems |
| Weobly | woobly |
| Wey | wā |
| Whitehaven | whittan |
| Whittingham | whittinjam |

## ENGLAND, SCOTLAND, AND
## IRELAND—Continued.

| | |
|---|---|
| Whoulsicke | hole-syke |
| Wildboarclough | wilbercluf |
| Wilhampstead | wilstead |
| Wilmslow | wimslow |
| Wirksworth | wirsydy |
| Wistaston | wistesson |
| Witham | wittn |
| Withington | withiton |
| Wiverton | wirton |
| Wolseley | woolzy |
| Wolstanston | ushitn |
| Wolverhampton | wolverton |
| Wombwell | wombel |
| Woodfardisworthy | oolsery |
| Wooddale | woodle |
| Woolwich | woolich |
| Worfield | wurvel |
| Wrotham | rootum |
| Wybemburg | wimbry |
| Yardley | ardly |
| Yeovil | yovil |
| Youghal | yoh-hil |
| | yowl |

# OCEANICA.

| | |
|---|---|
| Adelie | ah-deh-lee′ |
| Ahii | I-yee′ |
| Aijerbangis | I-yer-bang′-ghees |
| Aijoe | I′-yow |
| Ailu | I-loo′ |
| Aitaki | I-tah′-kee |
| Ampunam | ahm-poo′-nahm |
| Anjer | ahn′-yer |
| Atauai | ah-tŏw-I′ |
| Bassein | bahs-sāne′ |
| Benculen | ben-koo′-len |
| Bezoeki | beh-zoo′-kee |
| Ceicer de Mer | sā-sair′-deh-mair′ |
| Ceiram | sā rownh′ |
| Chantobon | shahn-to-bun′ |
| Chichia | chee′-chee-a |
| Cockburn | cŏ′-burn |
| Coepang | coo′-pang |
| Coetivy | co-et-ee′-vee |
| Cuivre | kweevr′ |
| Culebra | coo-lā′-bra |
| Daauw | dŏw |
| Eaheinomawe | ā ah-hI-no-mŏw′-eh |
| Eimeo | I-mā′-o |
| Goentoe | goon-too′ |
| Guguan | goo-gwahn′ |
| Hapaii | hap-pI′-ee |
| Hawaii | hāh-wI′-ee |
| Hivaoa | ee-vah-o′-a |
| Hoellalioe | hoo′-lah-lee-oo′ |
| Huahina | hoo-ah-hee′-nah |
| Jackinot | zhah-kee no′ |
| Kaihoolawe | kI-hoo-lah′-we |
| Kaipara | kI-pah′-rah |
| Katbalogan | kaht-bahl-o-gahn′ |
| Kauai | kŏw-I′ |
| Kediri | keh-dee′-ree |
| Kerguelen | kerg′-e-len |
| Kilauea | kee-lŏw-ā′-ah |
| Leyta | lā′-tah |
| Lifu | lee-foo′ |

## OCEANICA—Continued.

| | |
|---|---|
| Lochoe | loo-hoo′ |
| Loesa | loo′-sah |
| Macquarie | mak-kwor′-ree |
| Maitea | mī-tā′-ah |
| Manawatu | mah-nah-wah′-too |
| Maui | mŏw′-ee |
| Mauna Kea | mŏw′-nah-kā′-ah |
| Maapiti | mŏw-pee′-tee |
| Mawrua | mŏw-roo′-ah |
| Merapi | mā rah′-pee |
| Mindanao | mĭn-dah-nah′-o |
| Molokai | mo-lo-kī′ |
| Nihau | nee-hŏw′ |
| Oahtooak | o-ah-too-ahk′ |
| Oahu | o-ah′-hoo |
| Otago | o-tah′-go |
| Otaha | o′-tah-hah |
| Otou | o-too′ |
| Ouleai | oo-lā-ī′ |
| Ovolau | o-vo-lŏw′ |
| Pakuratahi | pah-koo-rah-tah′-hee |
| Palembang | pah-lem-bang′ |
| Papeiti | pāh-pā-ee′-tee |
| Patany | pah-tah′-nee |
| Patj tan | paht-yee-tahn′ |
| Quinhon | keen-hŏn′ |
| Quiuiluban | kee nee-loo-bahn′ |
| Radack | rah-dahk′ |
| Raiatea | rī-ah-tā′-ah |
| Ralick | rah-lik |
| Ranai | rah-nī′ |
| Raraka | rah-rah′-kah |
| Ruapehu | roo-ah-pā-hoo |
| Rua Wahine | roo′-ah-wah-hee′-neh |
| Samar | sah-mar′ |
| Samarang | sah-mah rahng′ |
| Savaii | sah-vī′ee |
| Seiuni | sāne-nee′ |
| Serayoe | seh-rī-yoo′ |
| Soembawa | soom-bŏw′-wah |
| Soerabayoe | soo-rah-bī′-yoo |
| Sungao | soon-gah′-o |
| Tahiti | tah-hee′-tee |
| Tahwata | tah-wah′-tah |
| Tairabu | tī-rah-boo′ |
| Taponamoa | tah-po-nah-mō′-ah |

## OCEANICA—Continued.

| | |
|---|---|
| Tapeantana | tah-pā-ahn-tah' nah |
| Taupo | tŏw-po |
| Tavai Poenamoo | tah-vī-poo-nah-moo' |
| Ternate | ter-naht' |
| Tewywys | teh-wee'-wees |
| Tyringin | tee-reen-gheen' |
| Tinian | tee-nee-ahn' |
| Tjanjor | tyahn-yor' |
| Tjidani | tyee-dah'-nee |
| Tjilatjap | tyee-laht-yahp' |
| Tjimanok | tyee-mah-nōk' |
| Tjitaroem | tyee-tah-room' |
| Tongariro | ton-gah-ree'-ro |
| Tontoli | ton-to'-lee |
| Toobonai | too-bo-nī' |
| Tubai | too-bī' |
| Tubuai Manu | too-boo-I'-mah-noo' |
| Tutuilla | too too-eel'-lah |
| Yahuga | oo-ah-hoo'-gah |
| Ualan | oo-ah-lahn' |
| Ulie | oo'-lee |
| Upolu | oo-po-loo' |
| Vavao | vah-vah'-o |
| Viti Levu | vee'-tee lā'-voo |
| Vuna | voo'-nah |
| Waiheki | wī-hā'-kee |
| Waiho | wī-ho' |
| Waikato | wī-kah'-to |
| Waikua | wī-koo'-ah |
| Waipa | wī-pah' |
| Wairarapa | wī-rah-rah'-pah |
| Waiwairoa | wī-wī-rō'-ah |
| Wajo | wah'-yo |
| Wakatane | wah-kah-tah'-neh |
| Wanganui | wahn-gah-noo'-ee |
| Wangari | wah-gah'-ree |
| Wangerou | wahn-gah-roo' |
| Wangaruru | wahn-gah-roo'-roo |
| Waurekauri | waw-reh-kŏw-ree' |
| Yewndoun | yoon-doon |

# WELSH.

| | | | |
|---|---|---|---|
| a = a | in ah | Cadwaladr | cahd-oo.ahl-ahdr |
| | | Aber | ah-ber |
| i = ee | in bee | Ithel | ee-thel |
| | | Hir | heer |
| -u.⁴ = ĭ | in pin | Rhuddlan | rhith′-lan |
| | | Guttyn | ghit′-tön |
| -u = ee | in bee | Cwmdu | koom′-dee |
| | | Teulu | toi-lee |
| w = oo | in boot | Bottwnog | bot-too′-nog |
| | | Cwm | koom |
| -y- = ö=u | in fur | Myrddin | mör-thin |
| | | Mynwy | mön′-oo-ee |
| -y = ee | in bee | Llaety | hlī′-tee |
| | | Eiry | ī′-ree |
| | | | |
| ae = I | in pine | Cattraeth | caht′-rīthe |
| | | Maen | mīne |
| ai = I | in pine | Braic-Y-Pwll | brīke-ee-poohl |
| | | Mechain | meh′-ch-hīne¹ |
| au = oi | in coin | Dauddwr | doi-thoor |
| | | Dyvynaul | dö-vö-noil |
| aw = öw | in cow | Madawc | mah-döwc |
| | | Mawr | möwr |
| ei = I | in pine | Llanddeiniolen | hllan-thī-nee o′-len |
| | | Einion | ī′-nee on |
| eu = oi | in coin | Llanbeulan | hllan-boi′-lan |
| | | Aneurin | ah-noi′-rin |
| iw = ū | in tune | Lyglyw | lög′-lū |

## WELSH—Continued.

| | | | |
|---|---|---|---|
| yw = ū | in tune | Llywelyn | hlū-el'-lön |
| | | Hywel | hū'-el |
| oe = oi | in coin | Coed-Y-Cumar | koïd-ee-kih'-mar |
| | | Kyvoesi | kö-voi'-see |
| c = k | | Caer | kire |
| | | Cwm | koom |
| ch[1] = ch-h | | Abererch | ah-ber-erch-h[1] |
| | | Gwladgarwch | goo-lahd- gar-ooch-h[1] |
| dd = th | in the | Eisteddfod | ice-teth-fod |
| | | Gwenddwr | goo-en'-thoor |
| f = v | | Llanfair | hllan-vīre |
| | | Mathafarn | mah-thah-varn |
| ff = f | | Dyffryn | döf'-frön |
| | | Gryffydd | grö'-föth |
| g[2] = g | in get | Gwgan | goo'-gan |
| | | Gyveurydd | gö voi'-röth |
| ll[3] = hl-l | | Llanveithin | hllan-vī'-thin |
| | | Llywarch | lū'-arch-h |
| th = th | in thud | Mathafarn-Eithaf | mah-thah'-varn-I'-thav |

1. *ch* is an aspirate guttural best pronounced after a broad *ah*.
2. *-g-* is the same guttural vocalized. 3. *ll* is *l* prolonged and aspirate,
so that while the tongue still touches the roof of the mouth, the
breath passes forcibly on each side. 4. A hyphen after a letter,
before it, or both before and after it, indicate its position as initial,
final, or in the middle of a word.

www.ingramcontent.com/pod-product-compliance
Lightning Source LLC
Chambersburg PA
CBHW020327090426
42735CB00009B/1440